# When Faith Goes Viral

# When Faith Goes Viral

*11 Success Stories of the New Evangelization
From Alabama to Vladivostok*

Edited by Philip F. Lawler

*A Herder & Herder Book*
The Crossroad Publishing Company
New York

The Crossroad Publishing Company
www.CrossroadPublishing.com

© 2013 by Philip F. Lawler

All rights reserved. No part of this book may be reproduced, stored in a retrieval system, or transmitted, in any form or by any means, electronic, mechanical, photo-copying, recording, or otherwise, without the written permission of The Crossroad Publishing Company.

The stylized crossed letter C logo is a registered trademark of The Crossroad Publishing Company.

Printed in the United States of America.
ISBN 978-08245-49824 (alk. paper)

Library of Congress Cataloging-in-Publication Data available from the Library of Congress.

Cover design by George Foster.

All biblical citations in this chapter are taken from the Catholic Edition of the Revised Standard Version of the Bible, copyright 1965, 1966 by the Division of Christian Education of the National Council of the Churches of Christ in the United States of America. Used by permission. All rights reserved.

In continuation of our 200-year tradition of independent publishing, The Crossroad Publishing Company proudly offers a variety of books with strong, original voices and diverse perspectives. The viewpoints expressed in our books are not necessarily those of The Crossroad Publishing Company, any of its imprints or of its employees. No claims are made or responsibility assumed for any health or other benefit.

Books published by The Crossroad Publishing Company may be purchased at special quantity discount rates for classes and institutional use. For information, please email sales@crossroadpublishing.com.

## Praise for *When Faith Goes Viral*

Effective evangelization is a crucial question for the Church and it's good to see that Philip Lawler, an experienced and fair-minded journalist, has turned his attention to studying and highlighting programs that actually work.

Robert Royal, president, Faith & Reason Institute,<br>and author, *The God That Did Not Fail*

Phil Lawler is a man of many talents, and among them is the ability to dig out the truth even when it hurts. But this latest work is quite the opposite—it is the kind of book that makes one want to run out and celebrate all that is new and exciting in the world of evangelization. A real shot in the arm, this book is a must-read.

Judie Brown, President, American Life League

Phil Lawler is one of the most trusted Catholic journalists in the world today. Without fear or favor, he reports what is troubling in the Church, but he also pursues, as in this book, her points of light.

George Neumayr, Contributing Editor,<br>*The American Spectator*,<br>and Coauthor, *No Higher Power*

Phil Lawler has specialized for so long in bad news, it's nice to see that he's found some good news this time. And his reputation for accuracy makes the reader more confident that these encouraging stories are the real thing.

Jim Holman, Editor, *San Diego Reader*,<br>and Publisher, *California Catholic Daily*

His own writings show Philip Lawler to be an exceptionally lucid and graceful essayist. Events in the life of the Church have shown him to be one of the most perspicuous analysts of the contemporary situation. This latest work will advance his reputation both as a writer and as an observer of extraordinary shrewdness.

Rev. Paul Mankowski, SJ<br>Fellow in Residence, Lumen Christi Institute

Few US Catholics have written with as much balance and insight as Phil Lawler about what's wrong with the Church in America. That's why he just might be the best person alive to help the faithful see what the Church is doing right.

Rod Dreher<br>Senior Editor, *The American Conservative*

# Contents

Foreword: Winning the World, One Friend at a Time — ix

Introduction: Jesus Wrote No Memos — xxiii

Chapter One: Reaching the Hearts of College Students — 1

Chapter Two: Light for the East—The New Evangelization in Eastern Europe — 20

Chapter Three: Mother Angelica and the Founding of EWTN — 39

Chapter Four: Latin Americans Give Jesus for Christmas — 55

Chapter Five: Kenyan Street Kids Learn of Cows and Catechisms — 74

Chapter Six: Music Fuels a Catholic Rebirth in Vladivostok — 84

Chapter Seven: In Downtown Chicago,
a Liturgy Glimpses Eternity                             95

Chapter Eight: Persecuted Indian
Christians Evangelize . . . by Forgiving                111

Chapter Nine: Witness Without Words:
Evangelization Under Islam                              130

Chapter Ten: "For I Languish with Love":
Filling Up Those Empty Confessionals                    141

Chapter Eleven: First Adore, Then Evangelize            157

About the Author                                        181

**FOREWORD**

# Winning the World, One Friend at a Time

## C. John McCloskey III

"Christianity is true and the truth always has a future."
—Pope Benedict XVI[1]

"The Church is 'the natural home of the Human Spirit.'"
—G.K. Chesterton[2]

You hold in your hands a magnificent new book on the New Evangelization of Catholicism throughout the world—and one that comes most opportunely, as the Church completes the Year of Faith commemorating the beginning of the Second Vatican Council and the publication of the *Catechism of the Catholic Church*.

Philip Lawler has chosen to concentrate on the thriving global Catholic institutional initiatives that have flourished, particularly beginning with the singular pontificate of Blessed John Paul II.

However, as I like to put it, "if all politics is local then all Catholic apostolate is essentially personal." One must convert to Christ daily to be granted the graces to change the world, and generally changing the world takes place one person at a time.

As the *Catechism* reminds us, winning converts should be a constant concern for all Catholics: "The true apostle is on the lookout for occasions of announcing Christ by word, either to unbelievers . . . or to the faithful" (905). How then should we go about it? God pours out his saving grace in many ways, but he normally requires, and we could even say desires, the willing collaboration of his sons and daughters in this joyful task. The famous Catholic philosopher (and convert) Dietrich von Hildebrand said that we should look upon all people we encounter as Catholics *in re* (in fact) or *in spe* (potentially). I agree.

Admit it: Don't you from time to time think about sharing with your neighbor, your friend, your family member, your colleague, the joy that is in your heart, the fullness of our faith in the Catholic Church? Perhaps some of you have had the wonderful experience of being the godparent or sponsor of a friend whom, by God's grace, you have guided into the Church. You know then the joy of being God's instrument.

This delight is always a cause for holy celebration, but particularly in the present threatened circumstances of our culture. Has there ever in the Christian era been a more joyless, aimless, lonely society than our own, one which appears to have gained the whole world but has forgotten its own soul? On the other hand, have there ever been three consecutive Roman pontiffs who have so incessantly and hopefully proclaimed the Gospel in all its fullness, addressing the fallen yet redeemed world's hopes and anxieties so completely?

The infant Church's constant growth through its first three centuries of religious persecution occurred through the witness and personal influence of thousands of Christians and their families. In the centuries following Constantine's edict of toleration, Christian ideals lived out in the world gradually transformed the West into the form of Christian culture that we know as the Middle Ages. In our own time, in the wake of the titanic struggles of ideas and ideologies of the last two centuries (Darwinism, Marxism, Freudianism, and so on), we are called to do something similar. In fact, the partial success of these various heresies and ideologies has been due in part to a Catholic laity largely "missing in action" in the apostolic sense through the last several centuries, ignorantly content to let the clergy and religious do the "heavy lifting."

Here I aim to give some insights, largely based upon my own experience, into how we can more effectively spread the gift of faith through example and friendship:

what Blessed John Cardinal Newman referred to as the "apostolate of personal influence."

## A New Springtime

Pope John Paul believed that our entry into the third millennium marked our crossing the "threshold of hope" into "a new springtime for the Church." If this is to happen, it will depend ultimately on the apostolate of millions of persons and families. He went on to say in his letter on missionary activity: "Christ, whose mission we continue, is the 'witness' par excellence and the model of all Christian witness. The first form of witness is the very life of the missionary, of the Christian family, and of the ecclesial community."

We may refer to this sharing of our faith as evangelization, giving witness, etc. I prefer the word used most often by the Conciliar fathers in this regard, apostolate: The second Vatican Council tells us: "The individual apostolate, flowing generously from its source in a truly Christian life...admits of no substitutes. Regardless of status, all lay persons (including those who have no opportunity or possibility for collaboration in associations) are called to this type of apostolate and obliged to engage in it."[3]

In an apostolic exhortation on the laity by John Paul II, the point could not be made clearer:

> The entire mission of the Church, then, is concentrated and manifested in evangelization....
> In fact, the "good news" is directed to stirring

a person to a conversion of heart and life and a clinging to Jesus Christ as Lord and Savior; to disposing a person to receive Baptism and the Eucharist and to strengthen a person in the prospect and realization of new life according to the Spirit.[4]

In short, the buck stops with each one of us. "Every disciple is personally called by name; no disciple can withhold making a response: 'Woe to me if I do not preach the gospel'" (1 Cor 9:16).

A few words of caution. We are not speaking of proselytism (in the pejorative sense). That is to say, our sharing, witnessing, and so on must have absolutely nothing to do with coercion, or lack of respect for the "freedom of the children of God." Quite the contrary: we realize that only God's grace can effect a conversion and that pressure, other than our prayer, sacrifice, good example, and friendship, would not only in the long term certainly be counterproductive but would also not respect "the dignity of the human person" so central to the teachings of the Second Vatican Council and of Blessed John Paul II.

How then do we "make" converts? First of all, *we* don't; God does. What then is our first step in proposing that someone consider becoming a Catholic? Naturally the desire will flow out of our prayer life. We come into contact with dozens if not hundreds of people in the course of our daily lives each month, ranging from dearest family members and intimate friends to the butcher, baker, and candlestick maker. We look at them and ask ourselves: "Could this person be open to our faith?" If the answer is yes, on to the next step.

## Why Not Ask?

It is said that the most effective way to raise money for a good cause is to simply ask for it. The same may be applied to our situation. The question "Have you ever thought of becoming a Catholic?" addressed to many people over the course of our life, will certainly produce not only converts but also interesting and thought-provoking conversations and new personal relationships. You may have to practice this line in front of a mirror a few times, just as you did before asking out your first date. You generally will be surprised at how flattered, if somewhat surprised, people are by the question.

Naturally we are not approaching perfect strangers. Indeed, if we are not in the process of developing a deep and lasting friendship with the potential new member of the Church, then our question lacks authenticity and will be rightfully judged as impertinent and insincere.

When you pose that question, the great majority of people will reply that you are the first person who has ever asked them. More than a few will add that they have been waiting for someone to ask them that question all their lives! A few will react negatively, but after all, not all "have eyes to see or ears to hear." We "shake the dust off our feet" and go on. We are driven not by the need for success, but by the "love of Christ that compels us." And we may eventually be surprised after the passage of time, even many years, that people come back to us looking for answers because we once had the courage to offer them the faith.

We are challenging people to consider making the most significant decision they will ever make in their lives, infinitely more important than the choice of school, profession, or spouse. It is essential that you get to know them well, particularly their religious background, if any, so you will "know where they are coming from." Of use in this regard would be a thorough reading of *Separated Brethren*, a survey of Protestant, Anglican, Eastern Orthodox, and other denominations in the United States by William J. Whalen. By engaging in conversation on the question of religious faith, you will be inviting your friend, and committing yourself, to go deep below the surface of everyday trivialities into the heart of the matter: Why are we here? What is truth? Is there a right and wrong? Is there a God? An afterlife? Is Jesus Christ God? Did he found a Church during his lifetime? If so, which one? Do we need to belong to it to be saved?

## Be Prepared

Of course, you need to be not only willing to discuss and answer these queries but prepared to do so. "Be ready always with an answer to everyone who asks a reason for the hope that is in you" (1 Pet 3:15). To be fully prepared is the work of a lifetime, but that does not excuse us from evangelizing while we learn on the job. Remember, no matter how little we know, our friends usually know less. And we at least know where to go for the answers. In fact, a lot of our catechetical work with our potential convert friends will simply take the form of referring them to the best sources.

Obviously we should have a good grasp of the New Testament and the *Catechism of the Catholic Church*, our fundamental texts. However, ideally we should also slowly but surely read and study the great English and American apologists: John Henry Newman, C. S. Lewis, G. K. Chesterton, Robert Hugh Benson, and Ronald Knox and the more modern masters, Frank Sheed and Peter Kreeft. Many of their works are in print. It is also useful to become familiar with the magisterial teachings of the Pope for the most current guidance on matters of faith and morals.

Reviewing our own preparation leads directly to the question of recommending reading for friends who express an interest in our faith. An increasing number of people simply don't understand the basic vocabulary of what it means to believe. For friends interested in an intellectual approach, an excellent brief volume is *Belief and Faith* by the famous German philosopher Josef Pieper. He draws heavily on Blessed Cardinal Newman's much more complex *Grammar of Assent*.

Many people even today need a book to awaken their interest in Christianity or help make Christianity "reasonable" and understandable. Several books come immediately to mind. Both *Orthodoxy* and *The Everlasting Man* by Chesterton will stimulate the reader. I am thinking also of a basic primer, *A Map of Life* by Frank Sheed, and C. S. Lewis' famous *Mere Christianity*. Most fundamental, of course, is the New Testament. An excellent version with ascetical commentary is *The Navarre Bible*. And I recommend a good life of Christ (try those by Alban Goodier, Fulton Sheen, Giuseppe Riccioti, or Romano Guardini). After all, your friends need to meet the man if they are ever to join his Church.

Next is a good catechism, to help them come to know the Church and her teachings. In the last few decades there have been many excellent new ones or updates of older ones based on the sound teaching of the Church updated to reflect the Second Vatican Council and the *Catechism of the Catholic Church*. Authors to look for include Ronald Lawler, Leo Trese, John Hardon, and John Noll.

I recommend that you whet people's appetite for conversion with a book or two of conversion stories, such as *Spiritual Journeys* (Pauline Publications) or *Surprised by Truth* (Basilica Press). Our friends will likely be drawn to read about the contemporary conversion stories of so many people drawn to the faith from such varied backgrounds and are likely to find at least part of their own story in one of these narratives.

Don't forget, either, classic spiritual autobiographies like those of St. Augustine, Blessed John Henry Cardinal Newman, Thomas Merton, and Malcolm Muggeridge—and the more recent offering by the late former abortionist and convert to the Catholic faith Dr. Bernard Nathanson, *The Hand of God* (Life Cycle Books). They have changed millions of hearts and minds.

You should also familiarize your friends with the richness of the history of the Church, where they can see the continuity of the faith through the apostolic succession and read the dramatic story of evangelization through the centuries with its ups and downs. Here I would recommend Msgr. Philip Hughes's *Popular History of the Church* (Macmillan) for a short synopsis, and the first five volumes of the magisterial *History of Christendom* by Warren Carroll (Christendom College Press). The latter volumes read like novels, are painstakingly researched, and reveal the Church in all its heights and depths, complete with her saints and her sinners.

An important part of our work of introducing our friends to the faith will be exposing them to the beauty of the Catholic liturgy and to the art, literature, and music of Catholic inspiration. Accompanying them to Holy Mass and other liturgical events, such as the celebration of solemn benediction, a baptism, a wedding, the Easter vigil, an episcopal consecration, the ordination of new priests, or a rosary pilgrimage to a shrine of the Virgin can bring them to a deep appreciation of the incarnate aspect of our faith and its sacramental nature. To listen to Gregorian chant (today so surprisingly popular) or the great classical compositions centered on the Mass, the Psalms, or various events in the life of Christ and

Our Lady, will also draw them closer to the heart of the Church.

Those who love great literature can be deeply moved by an introduction to the great Catholic authors, starting with Dante, continuing on down the centuries to Alessandro Manzoni and Henryk Sienkiewicz in the nineteenth century, and to Sigrid Undset, Evelyn Waugh, Flannery O'Connor, George Bernanos, François Mauriac, Walker Percy, and Shusako Endo in the twentieth. These artists each, in his own way, captures the divine in the human.

But let's be realistic. Not all of your friends, by any means, will be receptive to so heavily intellectual an approach. You may need to be much more selective in what you recommend: pamphlets rather than books, Catholic hymns rather than symphonies, a more contemporary (although sound) version of the New Testament rather than the Douay-Rheims, the stained glass in your parish church rather than Chartres. Listen to their needs and their questions and try to satisfy them. Time spent in prayer with them or a visit to poor or elderly people may prove much more influential in drawing them towards the Church than any possible reading you might give them.

## Teamwork and Persistence

Let's not forget the parish and the priest. After all, if all goes well, your friend will likely spend the rest of his life normally worshipping in a parish setting. If your friend has not been baptized, the Church normally asks that the budding catechumen be enrolled in the R.C.I.A. program (Rite of Christian Initiation of Adults) in his local parish, which will take him through a month-by-month program of initiation that culminates normally in Baptism during the Easter Vigil (hopefully with you there as his godparent). If he has been baptized, he will make his first Confession and then receive the sacrament of Confirmation and first Holy Communion within a Mass on Easter or at another time.

If possible, it is useful and proper to establish a team approach in dealing with your friends. Find a prayerful, zealous (they really are synonymous) priest with whom you can work and triangulate—which is to say that both of you working together can offer your insights and wisdom, your prayer and sacrifice to your friend. The priest may be able, perhaps, to enter better into some areas that you cannot. He will also be able to advise you about the best way and moment for your friend to be incorporated in the Church, taking careful notice of personal circumstances.

What happens if over a reasonable amount of time your friend just doesn't "get it?" He claims he doesn't see it. His difficulties with Christ and the teachings of the Church still result in doubt. His family, parents, and spouse present what appear to be insuperable obstacles. Do you throw him overboard in order to sail off for other prizes? You wouldn't think of it! The answer is prayer, persistence, and patience. The violence of your prayer (remember Who is in charge of this operation) will eventually bear him away. Your persistence and constancy in true friendship will eventually win him over by showing that your love is unconditional. Remember: you may be the one person in his life who is interested only in his salvation. No ulterior motives of any sort. By patience we show our realization that conversion takes place at God's pace, not a minute sooner or later. The conversion may not happen until he is on his deathbed, and you may witness it from heaven.

Or else he does "get it," and enters the Church. What now? Naturally your apostolic efforts will be focusing on the next person, or perhaps you are already dealing with several people at the same time. However, don't forget your newborn Catholic friend. He is just a very young child in the faith, taking his first tottering steps into a bright new world that will have its storms and shadows. Some who regard Catholicism and his conversion to it, in Chesterton's words, as "a nuisance and a new and a dangerous thing" will surround him. He needs nurturing, your encouragement, your friendship, and your support.

St. Josemaría Escrivá says, "Sanctification is the work of a lifetime." As your friend's godfather, sponsor, or guide, you have to be with him every step of the way. Perhaps you will introduce him to other institutions and spiritualities of the Church that can further his spiritual progress. Whatever the path in the Church he takes, he will be eternally grateful to you. And you in your turn will echo the words of a famous French convert and poet, Paul Claudel, who said, "Tell him his only duty is to be joyful."

*C. John McCloskey, III, STD is a priest of the Prelature of Opus Dei, and the former Catholic chaplain at Princeton University. He currently is Research Fellow of the Faith and Reason Institute in Washington, DC.*

INTRODUCTION

# Jesus Wrote No Memos

*Philip F. Lawler*

Those of us who make our living by writing are sometimes tempted to believe that any problem can be solved by brilliant prose. If we could only produce that one truly brilliant work of apologetics, we suspect, the entire world would be converted.

Not so. We have it on the highest authority—I should say, the Highest Authority—that writing is not the most effective way to convey the faith. The Gospels show our Lord writing only once (John 8:6): scratching in the dirt with his finger, clearly not intending to produce a permanent record of his thoughts. In fact there is no permanent record of Christ's words, except as they were recorded by others. He chose not to write an autobiography, but to let his disciples tell us about him.

Jesus might even have prepared detailed, personalized instructions for his apostles—or for that matter, for every Christian in history—on how to spread the Gospel message. Instead he told his apostles, "Go into all the world and preach the Gospel to the whole creation" (Mark 16:15), and left them to puzzle out how best that should be done.

Two thousand years later we are still puzzling over the question of how we should approach our task of evangelization. It is clear that Jesus intended for each one of us to pass along the faith; it is not at all clear how we should do this. There is no sales manual for Christianity.

There is the Bible, of course. But the Bible has very little influence if it is sitting on a shelf gathering dust. How we do, as believers, persuade someone to pick up the Bible? How do we introduce our neighbors to the Gospel?

The Scriptures do provide clues, cues, and examples for would-be evangelists. The familiar opening of St. John's Gospel, for example, tells us that "the Word became flesh and dwelt among us" (John 1:14). The Word of God is not a plan but a Person. We are not trying to persuade our neighbors to undertake some sort of self-help program (although conversion will surely help them); we are introducing them to Jesus Christ.

When did the process of evangelization begin? In that same opening chapter of his Gospel, St. John writes how St. Andrew reacted when he encountered Jesus: "He first found his brother Simon, and said to him, 'We have found the Messiah' (which means Christ). He brought him to Jesus" (John 1:41–42).

There it is: the first recorded occasion on which one of Christ's followers brought another to meet him. And what a beginning! My friend Father C. John McCloskey, Jr., who has graciously contributed the Foreword for this book, has earned an enviable reputation for bringing high-profile converts into the Catholic Church. But even he cannot begin to match the impact of St. Andrew's catch. Thanks to St. Andrew, his brother was in the upper room when the Holy Spirit descended on that first Pentecost Sunday, and St. Peter could deliver the powerful testimony that produced 3,000 baptisms in a single day.

The faith went viral on that Pentecost Sunday. The language of an Internet sensation can apply neatly to a successful program of evangelization. Sometimes a clever thought is posted online, draws a few appreciative chuckles, and disappears into cyberspace. But then sometimes an equally clever remark captures the imagination of readers, who share it. It tickles the fancy of others, who share it with still more people. So too the process of evangelization begins with a single act of witness: St. Andrew speaks to St. Peter, or St. Peter speaks to a group, who are so convinced that they relay his message to their friends, who pass it on again—and soon the news reaches thousands of people, including many who would never have encountered the original source.

Still, as exciting as that process is, we are still left to wonder how it begins. What can we do? What are others doing that has consistently shown results?

This book is not a definitive answer to those questions. There are as many paths to successful evangelization as there are individual Christians. Every believer has a network of personal contacts, a field of possibilities for spreading the faith. The challenge for Christianity is not to devise one grand, overarching scheme to guide everyone's actions, but to activate every little network, encouraging many thousands of individual initiatives. Some, no doubt, will fail. Some will yield only modest results. But some will go viral. Since we cannot predict which efforts will be successful (more on that later), the most productive approach may be to encourage as many efforts as possible.

In collecting examples of successful ventures in evangelization for this book, I deliberately chose a diverse set of endeavors. I gave authors very little advice about presentation, in the expectation (fulfilled, I think) that they would write in contrasting styles. There are very few common threads running through the chapters that follow. Most readers, I suspect, will not be sympathetic toward all of the projects that are described. If you find one story uncongenial, feel free to skip over it and explore the next one. My goal was to suggest a wide variety of approaches, in the hope that a typical reader will find at least one that he might emulate or amend to suit his own circumstances. Perhaps the multiplicity of approaches in itself will serve to stimulate some creative new thoughts.

The first two chapters cover fairly straightforward programs: the Fellowship of Catholic University Students (FOCUS), which trains and supports missionaries on American college campuses; and the Language and Catechetical Institute, which performs a similar service for mission work in the countries of the former Soviet bloc. The two institutions face enormously different practical challenges, but in the end they are fighting the same battle against the aridity of a secularized environment.

For years, whenever I have spoken to American Catholic audiences, I have faced questions from the audience about the best hope for the future of the Church in the United States. I invariably reply that we have been trained to look for signs of spiritual renewal in the wrong places; we often don't notice the rays of hope because they are shining from unexpected directions. To illustrate my point, my favorite example is the Eternal World Television Network (EWTN). Who could possibly have anticipated that the world's largest Christian broadcasting empire would be founded by an impulsive nun with a long history of medical problems and no credentials broadcasting whatsoever? The American Catholic bishops took a much more "professional" approach, developing a proper business plan and investing many millions of dollars in their television plans. Yet today the bishops have absolutely nothing to show for their investment, while Mother Angelica produced the most startling evangelizing success of our time. This is a story worth hearing, and reflecting upon, frequently.

The next two chapters tell of more modest successes in Latin America and in Africa. In Peru, a lay movement saw an opportunity to build on the popular climate of goodwill that comes at Christmas time, and transform it into a genuine religious sentiment. The *Navidad es Jesús* program begins by supplying presents to needy children, and ends by supplying spiritual direction to the volunteers who collect the toys. In Kenya a young man—himself formed by a local program administered by Opus Dei—recounts how he provided practical help and moral guidance for slum children, with the help of an aging aunt who supplied the boys with work on her farm.

When I asked friends and colleagues to send me their own favorite examples of successful evangelization, a surprising number mentioned the "way of beauty"—the time-honored technique of drawing people toward Christian belief through the arts. Those suggestions reminded me of a case with which I was already familiar: a little chapter in the Russian Far East, where organ concerts were drawing hundreds of people to visit a Christian church for the first time, and the beauty of sacred music was provoking some listeners to inquire further about the faith.

Closer to home, a determined effort to promote beauty in architecture, music, and especially in the liturgy has helped save some parishes from extinction. Here is the story of one such parish's dramatic turnaround. At St. John Cantius, whose congregation had dwindled to 250 after the Polish Catholics who'd built it moved out to the suburbs, the writing was on the wall: The place seemed all but doomed. Then came a dynamic pastor with a deep sense of the ways in which beauty can preach the truth, who did what seemed impossible: he assembled a hardworking choir, revived the old Latin Mass, and attracted so many new worshipers that now the gorgeous old landmark is almost fully restored. The parish is drawing both conversions and vocations, and even publishing books about the liturgy.

In the United States we might meet with skepticism or even hostility from secularists; in many other countries our brethren face outright persecution. Yet even—or especially!—in those circumstances, Christians can bear effective witness to the Gospel. Thousands of Christian families were driven from their homes in India's Orrisa state by mob violence orchestrated by Hindu radicals. Yet now some Hindus, including some of the mob's participants, have been won to the faith by the courageous endurance of the Christians under persecution.

We Americans are also blessed with the freedom that allows us to speak openly about our faith. In other societies, particularly in the Islamic world, Christians are not so fortunate. So I have included a report by a pastor from a parish in the Arab world—written under a pseudonym, to avoid reprisals against his little Christian community—on the special difficulties of preaching the Gospel in a country where religious conversions are officially outlawed.

Since the goal of evangelization is to bring people into the sacramental life of the Catholic Church, our book closes with two chapters that are designed especially to encourage the use of the sacraments. The "Light is On for You" campaigns (known by different names in the different dioceses where they have been organized) have made it easy and attractive for lapsed Catholics to find their way back into confessionals. In that respect they are a prime example of the New Evangelization.

Along with the "way of beauty," the approach to evangelization most commonly recommended by my friends and colleagues was Eucharistic adoration. It would seem, at first glance, that private prayer, in a quiet chapel before the Blessed Sacrament, is far removed from the active work of spreading the faith. But appearances can be deceiving; remember that St. Thérèse of Lisieux, a cloistered nun, is a patron of missionary work. In my own informal survey, I have discovered that whenever a church undertakes a program of Eucharistic adoration, the parish experiences a surge of new vigor. It is impossible to predict what form this new life will take, but it will certainly come; I dare any reader to produce a contrary example. So I thought it appropriate to this book with a chapter on Eucharistic adoration and the benefits it brings.

This book, I hope, will provide readers with both the inspiration and the encouragement that will help them launch their own evangelizing efforts. Inspiration, because among the many different initiatives portrayed in the following chapters, there may be some that will spark the reader's imagination. Encouragement, because many of the projects described in this book had very humble origins. If they could do it, you can do it. You serve the same God, whose help is always there for the asking.

CHAPTER ONE

# Reaching the Hearts of College Students

*John Burger*

Here is a tale of two colleges: Campus A is a modest, static and stable Midwestern Catholic college with about 750 students, who come from not too far away to study things like biology and education. The party scene is strong, with rampant "binge drinking" and a significant "hook-up culture." Incoming freshmen are greeted with a "kegger," an event that consistently draws some 400 students year after year. The school's Catholic roots go back almost 150 years. Members of the religious order that founded the school still have a presence. But there's not much going on in the way of campus ministry, and while students imbibe the good life at house parties throughout the year, daily Mass on campus attracts only a dozen or so worshipers.

Campus B is a growing college with more than 1,700 students that is rediscovering its Catholic roots. The school has embraced *Ex Corde Ecclesiae*, Pope John Paul II's roadmap for truly Catholic higher education. Administrators have have promised (and planned) to make the school "one of the great Catholic colleges in America" by focusing on not only academic excellence but also a "thriving faith life." The spiritual side of that equation is already in full play. The student population is 80 percent Catholic. There are almost 100 Bible-study groups on campus, drawing some 600 willing students. Daily Mass attracts about 400 attendees, Sunday Mass some 1,400. Hundreds attend Eucharistic adoration, which is available twelve hours a day, five days a week on campus and 24/7 at a nearby parish. A major Catholic student organization hosts a luau at the beginning of each year, and although no alcohol is served, the event is well attended. So are many other alcohol-free events throughout the year. Although enrollment has been growing, the number of student disciplinary cases has been dropping. Students hail from some three dozen states, attracted not only by the college's particular academic strengths but also its Catholic identity. Campus ministry is active, with plenty of volunteer opportunities. Many students spend their vacations on mission trips to places like Iraq, Haiti, West Africa, and the inner city of New York.

Every January 22, some 260 students take an 18-hour bus trip to Washington, DC, for the March for Life.

Where are these two contrasting colleges? They're in the exact same place: Benedictine College in Atchison, Kansas. Campus A describes the school in the late 1990s; Campus B describes it today.

## Growth from the Grass Roots

What accounts for the sudden rebirth of Benedictine? There are several factors, including growing demand from students for more access to the sacraments and devotional practices, a concerted effort to refocus on the mission of the college, and the hiring of several solidly faithful senior staff. But a good part of the Benedictine revolution was started and led by a student organization: the Fellowship of Catholic University Students (FOCUS), which hosts the college luau. Benedictine College is where FOCUS had its start in 1998, and while FOCUS has had an impact on thousands of young men and women at dozens of colleges, Benedictine's transformation was among its first fruits.

FOCUS was the brainchild of Curtis Martin, who announced the new initiative in early 1997 on EWTN's *Mother Angelica Live*. His old friend Edward Sri—who had just started as a theology professor at Benedictine—saw the broadcast. But Martin had not yet tried his ideas out in a college setting. So Sri approached some likely students about starting the first FOCUS chapter at Benedictine. Sri and Martin planned a retreat for those students, and they found a cabin in the middle of nowhere in Kansas, for a stay in the middle of January.

"Curtis and I joke about it. We call it the coldest night *ever* on earth," Sri says. "The women's cabin had heat, but the men's didn't.... It was the coldest point of the year, but the Lord was up to something that was going to set a fire on campuses throughout the United States in years to come." Martin and Sri assumed that the project would begin the following year, but after the retreatants heard the vision for FOCUS they demanded: "We want to start *now*."

"Curtis said, 'Well, I live in Ohio, so I can't really help you guys start it directly, but Professor Sri is here; he can help you,'" Sri recounts. "I remember being a little surprised. I had my full time job, I was working on my doctoral dissertation. I had enough on my plate."

But start they did. Sri and Martin consulted by phone and wrote the Bible-study lessons, which Sri would deliver. Students like Wurtz also began leading Bible studies under Sri's guidance and evolved into the first student leaders—missionaries, as they are now known. Within a couple of months, there were sixty students engaged in FOCUS Bible studies at Benedictine.

### Filling a Vacuum

The idea for FOCUS goes back to Martin's own college days—a time when, he recalls, he was "pretty absorbed in the culture and pretty far away from Christ," as a largely nominal Catholic. He went off to Louisiana State University packing a Bible, but only because his mother had insisted on it. He was flipping idly through it one day in his freshman year, and the reading drew him in. It began to change him. He found that he "rediscovered the person of Jesus Christ." He was struck by Luke 6:46 in particular: a passage in which Jesus says to his disciples, "Why do you call me 'Lord, Lord' and don't do what I say?"

"I had no response," says Martin. "I realized I was living an inconsistent life."

He was befriended by evangelical Protestants who taught him that Christianity is not a set of rules but a relationship with God. Martin became involved in Cru (formerly Campus Crusade for Christ). He told a friend that he was trying to fix his life up so he could follow Christ. "He said, 'You're never going to get your life fixed up enough to start following him. You have to *give* you life to him, and he will help you straighten your life out.'

"So I gave my life to Christ in my sophomore year and essentially said, 'I've made a mess of my life. I don't deserve you, but if you'll have me I will go wherever you lead me and do whatever you ask me.' And I've been trying to be true to that ever since."

For a while, Martin blamed the Catholic Church for his "inability to follow Christ as a young man." In time, he came to read the Church Fathers and "discovered they were Catholic and realized that they weren't going to convert, so I had to." Still, while he was involved in Cru, he witnessed a systematic outreach to college students by

Protestants. "Their work on campus had a huge impact on my life," Martin says.

Michaelann Martin, Curtis's wife, remembers how Curtis wondered why there wasn't something like Cru for Catholics. "God just sort of put it on his heart to start a Catholic organization to encourage faithful Catholic students to remain Catholic and to call other college students who are searching, to call them to the fullness of truth."

Certainly there are Newman Centers, Catholic campus ministries and local parishes for Catholic college students, "but there's no evangelical outreach" to college students on the part of the Catholic Church, Martin says. "FOCUS fits into that gap."

"Curtis was aware of the good things our Protestant brothers and sisters were doing," Sri says. "He was also aware of their shortcomings. I think he was trying to take the good that could be found in groups like Campus Crusade [and other groups] and bring them into a Catholic context. FOCUS always works with the local parish, the local campus ministry, with the blessing of the bishop, in line with Catholic principles."

FOCUS and similar groups face an uphill slog. Even at a Catholic college like Benedictine, young people are frequently caught up in a culture that leaves God on the margins. Pop culture hedonism and intellectual relativism combine to make moral and intellectual virtues hard to practice—or even recognize. Msgr. Stuart Swetland, vice-president at

Mount St. Mary's University in Emmitsburg, Maryland, and a regional chaplain for FOCUS, sums up the problem:

> The eighteen- to twenty-five year-old period is so vital in our efforts of pastoral care and evangelization. Most people…have to make the faith their own. They're still living with an inherited faith. Most people make their most significant life relationships, most important friendships at that age. They make vocational decisions. If we keep people in the Church and deepen their relationship with the Lord and the Church, we have them for life. If we lose them, it's very difficult to get them back.

And yet, if the Church is "hemorrhaging" young people of college age, as Martin notes, the university is the best place to reach out to them. "No place gathers people like the university," Martin says. "American universities have people from every country in the world. You can reach the entire world."

## Heart Speaks to Heart

The work of evangelization that FOCUS does is largely based on relationships. It begins with the missionary's friendship with God, which he tries to share by befriending the students he serves. Missionaries, who are not much older than those students, are expected to frequent the sacraments and make a daily holy hour before the

Blessed Sacrament. As FOCUS literature instructs them: "You talk to God about college students for an hour, and for the rest of the day you talk to college students about God." Martin explains: "We're praying for the people we lead in Scripture study. If we're not praying, our success will be illusory." That message trickles down to the FOCUS volunteers on campus. "The relationship with Jesus is so important. We can't give to people what we don't have," says Shannon Zurcher, a missionary at the University of Connecticut.

A typical FOCUS team at a college or university consists of four missionaries—two men and two women, who make their preparation at a five-week training session over the summer. On campus they reach out to invite students into small Bible-study groups, leading the sessions themselves and training other students to do the same.

Initial outreach to students is conducted in a variety of ways, including large social events and retreats as well as "dorm storming," in which team members simply knock on dormitory doors, introduce themselves, give out cookies, tell students what time Mass is, and ask if they are interested in Bible study. That direct approach resulted in more than 70 people signing up for Bible study the first year of FOCUS activity at Columbia University, reports Leah Sedlacek, one of the missionaries there. "There were 188 students at the first Sunday Mass [of the academic year] last year."

Another method is something David Trotter calls the "truth survey." Trotter, FOCUS' director of collegiate outreach for the Southern Plains region, explains. "The idea is to help them start thinking about the bigger questions in life, and particularly asking, 'Who is the person of Jesus Christ?' It opens the door for a deep conversation that led to them wanting to look into what Catholics believe and why they believe it. And our hope in that is to be able to engage students who are no longer practicing the faith, but also students who come from a variety of backgrounds who have never taken the time to look at what we believe as Catholics."

## Friendship First

Missionaries seek to enter students' lives, hoping the students eventually will enter the life of Christ. It's important to be *with* people, in more than one sense, before you share the Gospel with them. This is exemplified by the Gospel story of Christ meeting the woman at the well. Jesus and the woman talked about water before talking about how a supernatural thirst can be quenched forever.

"It's meeting people where they're at," explains Jeremy Rivera, a former Protestant pastor who is now director of communications at FOCUS headquarters outside Denver. "People choosing to live, to share Jesus with others, and are radically available to the students."

"A lot of it is like getting into students' lives—eating with them, playing volleyball, hanging out in dorms, going shopping together, building a relationship with them," says Zurcher. "That's what Jesus did. He got into his disciples' lives before he brought them into his Trinitarian life. We call it incarnational evangelization."

"As a missionary, I'm looking to find students to hang out with," says Amanda Pirih, a former team director who helped start FOCUS groups at the University of Illinois in Chicago in 2008 and New York University in 2009. "I go into the café, the coffee shop, the cafeteria. I bring my lunch, sit down at a random table and ask if I can join them, introduce myself, tell them what I'm doing on campus. I ask about them, just to…learn who they are. Most often it's not like recruiting people but growing friendships."

Missionaries aim at cultivating true Christian friendship in a world where "'friends' mean how many you have on Facebook," she says. "What FOCUS does so well is relational evangelization," says Father Brian Larkin, a priest of the Archdiocese of Denver who discerned his vocation through FOCUS. "Everyone is hungry for a relationship, wants to be loved."

Bible-study groups examine themes such as salvation history, scriptural apologetics, Christ-like leadership, and how to effectively share the faith. Although the Bible studies are "very well prepared with materials that are age-specific to college students, with historical background," the gatherings are "not supposed to be an intellectual pursuit," says Father Dan O'Reilly, campus minister at

Columbia University in New York. "It's designed to help students be in contact with the word of the Lord."

The groups also introduce students to the practice of *lectio divina*—the prayerful reading of Scripture—and Ignatian meditation, where one puts oneself into the scene in a particular passage of the Bible, bringing the Scriptures more to life and leading to a greater appreciation for what God wants to say to the heart of the Christian in prayer.

"I have to let Jesus speak to me in silence. That's what really changes people's hearts, bringing them to prayer and letting them know how to do that," says Shannon Zurcher. "I tell people I'm not the one who will be teaching you; you really have to learn from Jesus."

The missionaries invite some of the students in Bible study—those who demonstrate special potential—into a mentoring relationship known as discipleship. "If one particular student is really responding to the stuff we're learning and wants to go deeper, I pray about asking this person into discipleship," Pirih says. She compares discipleship, a one-to-one relationship, to the last three years of Christ's life. "Our Lord went camping with twelve men for three years," she says—a time in which those twelve were learning the mysteries of the Kingdom of God and being formed to carry out the Great Commission. The missionary and the disciple pursue holiness together. "We meet for Mass, grab a cup of coffee, talk about life, about relationships."

Discipleship also is a time of deeper Scripture study so the disciple can begin leading Bible-study groups of his own, says Luke Oestman, the FOCUS team leader at Franciscan University in Steubenville.

This very personal, one-one-one approach might be slow, but it's sure. "In talking to Curtis once, he said numbers don't matter," recalls Peter Droege, former editor of the *Denver Catholic Register* and a longtime FOCUS supporter. "You could have 300 people show up at an event, but if behaviors don't change you haven't accomplished much. The approach is discipleship, to really form the missionaries in their faith. In turn, they form others in their faith etc. Jesus would send disciples out two-by-two. If two catechize four people, they in turn catechize eight, and so on." Martin calls it "spiritual multiplication," a process in which one committed Catholic works with a handful of others, trains them and sends them out to do the same. "In FOCUS they'd say 'You can be something to everyone or you could be everything to someone. Depth is better than breadth," says Father Larkin.

## Forced to Be Generous

But before any of this can happen, FOCUS has to be invited to campus. That invitation comes from the university chaplain, who must first obtain approval from his bishop. The chaplaincy agrees to pay $50,000 a year for four missionaries (two men and two women), which is roughly 20 percent of what it costs to recruit, train, house and manage them. FOCUS raises the rest, and missionaries help by finding their own sponsors. "The 20 percent is probably what [the chaplain] would pay for one full-time campus minister, but we're able to give him four, who are well-trained and close to the age of the students," says Sean Dalton, who, as FOCUS' regional director of the West, manages eleven campuses in South Dakota, Nebraska, Colorado, and Arizona.

Dalton says that the qualities FOCUS looks for in hiring missionaries are summed up in an acronym—FAITH: Faithfulness, Availability (two years minimum), Initiative, Teachability, and Heart. A potential missionary is someone who ready to devote himself to reaching people who have no interest in the faith, students who are wrapped up in the worldly distractions and confusions one finds on a typical college campus.

The FOCUS approach of cultivating friendships before evangelizing has yielded a lot of fruit. "Advice or counsel that comes from people who aren't your friends can sound judgmental," says Brian Lee, a seminarian at Mount St. Mary's Seminary in Emmitsburg, Maryland. Lee is one of eight former FOCUS missionaries who are now seminarians at the Mount. "People aren't going to start jumping in and believing what you say unless they know who you are."

"It's great for college students to have faithful Catholics they can look up to who aren't Mom and Dad," says Michaelann Martin (Curtis' wife) who has three sons at Benedictine and appreciates the fact that "they are around faithful FOCUS missionaries, young cool guys who love God and live their faith." Since they are close to students in age and sensibilities, FOCUS missionaries are "doing the outreach no priest or religious could do," says Msgr. Swetland. "They can meet with students at any time."

FOCUS played a role in helping Lee discern a vocation to the priesthood, as it did for Father Brian Larkin, who said that FOCUS "taught me how to give of myself. It challenged me in a way nothing else ever had done. It forced me to be generous, to say no to self so you could say yes to others."

"Part of the ethos in FOCUS, one of the five pillars, is heroic generosity," says Father Larkin, a priest of the Archdiocese of Denver. "Christ speaks of it quite a bit: 'He who would save his life would lose it.'" When he was a disciple in FOCUS, Larkin experienced that heroic generosity from his mentor, someone, he says, "who would always be there for me. . . . Anything I needed to talk about was on the table."

"Oftentimes it's seven at night and you're so tired, and there's one more student that calls, needing to talk," Father Larkin reported. Being prepared to answer those calls from students in need is good preparation, it would seem, for the priesthood—or for parenthood.

Another priest who can attribute his vocation largely to FOCUS is Father David Nix. FOCUS, he says, provided the best formation he had ever had in his life. In human terms, FOCUS uses "great Catholic leaders who want to be saints and heroes" to train its missionaries. Spiritually, Father Nix says, "it's expected that you not just go to Mass and confession and pray your rosary but that you actually enter into meditation.... You can't attain holiness without mental prayer, a lot of saints say. And the time in meditation and the holy hour, I think, places FOCUS above and beyond most other evangelization organizations, and possibly above the training of many in religious life."

Intellectually, FOCUS missionaries receive training from the likes of Hahn, Sri, and Tim Gray, a Scripture scholar who founded the Augustine Institute. Father Nix recalls FOCUS' emphasis on Scripture study also helps give it credence among many non-Catholic Christians who take pride in their knowledge of the Bible.

Pastorally, Father Nix says, FOCUS teaches the missionary how to reach people for Christ by being "extraordinary and normal at the same time—normal in the fact that you're accessible; extraordinary in the fact that there's something different about you.... That comes from being with people who desire to follow Christ very closely."

"FOCUS has given more priests to the Church than any other organization I can think of," Father Nix says. "Focus taught me how to love as a man ought to love," says Brian Lee, the seminarian. He was introduced to the theology of the body of Pope John Paul II, and two quotes from the Pope stuck with him. "In order to give oneself, one must first possess himself." And "Looking to another as a means to an end does violence to that very person." During his first year as a missionary, he meditated on those two quotes, "praying that I'd be able know I'm loved by him and be willing to accept what his call is for me." That and some healthy spiritual reading helped him to say Yes to the priestly vocation.

## Changing Lives

Jeremy Rivera counts 340 young people who, like Fathers Larkin and Nix and seminarian Lee, after their encounter with FOCUS, have decided to go into priesthood or religious life. One atheist came to know Christ through FOCUS and is now in formation with the Order of Preachers, according to Dominican Father John McGuire, former director at the Catholic Center at New York University, another campus where FOCUS is active.

There are countless other stories of young men and women who simply came to know Christ for the first time, returned to the Church, or deepened their spiritual life because of FOCUS. Missionaries past and present speak glowingly of having a "front seat" at the workings of the Holy Spirit in the lives of people they meet:

- A Columbia University student who was encouraged so much by the presence of FOCUS on campus that she bravely stood up to explain Catholic teaching on the Eucharist in front of a class, after a teacher mocked the doctrine as a "superstition."
- A student who went from being a "party girl" to someone who opened up to her friends about the dangers of such a lifestyle.

- A young woman who decided not to abort her baby and gave it up for adoption to a couple who could not conceive.

Shannon Zurcher says that FOCUS set her on a whole new path. As a student she had enjoyed "a typical college lifestyle, partying." She recalls: "I was never really into my faith, even though I went to Mass on Sundays, as I had growing up. But I never put my faith at the center of my life. I remember being unhappy at times. I cried when I came home from parties. I didn't really know there could be more in life." She met a fellow student who attended FOCUS events, and noticed that she "seemed way happier than I was. I met her as a freshman. I remember thinking 'People go to Mass during the week? That's so weird.'" The following year, she found her on Facebook and decided to call her.

"I desired to learn more about my faith. She was starting a Bible study. I saw the missionaries and the students involved as living a Christian life in a way I had never seen it before: the love for the Eucharist, or just like, evangelization—that's part of what Jesus asked us to do. It was attractive to me, and I wanted to be part of something great and something big."

In addition to the stories of individual lives changes, there is anecdotal evidence of FOCUS' effect on the larger community at particular institutions.

Father Dan O'Reilly reports that since FOCUS came to Columbia in 2011, Mass attendance has risen, and he has had a "steady stream of people coming to my office for confession…at least two or three people every day." And the quality of confessions is excellent, he says. "FOCUS missionaries help them with an examination of conscience." He also sees greater attentiveness to Scripture and intellectual curiosity stirred up by the Bible studies. "Often after Mass I get questions about the Scriptures or what more could I read about this."

"It's cool to see students come alive in their faith," says Zurcher. "When I meet them they're like nominally Catholic…When they realize they are made to be saints it's so cool to see."

## Steady Growth

The "fire" that FOCUS started continues to spread, slowly but steadily. By the fall 2012 semester, FOCUS had 361 missionaries working on seventy-four campuses. The apostolate was hopeful about adding another ten to fifteen campuses for the 2013-2014 year. Martin believes the effort will reach beyond the college years. FOCUS' motto is "Launching college students into lifelong Catholic mission." While FOCUS has engendered a fair number of religious vocations, most people touched by the apostolate will go on to marriage and family life, where they will have a chance to form their own children in the faith. They will also likely be active in their parishes. "They'll be teaching their own kids about the faith someday," Father O'Reilly explains. "It's something they will carry with them throughout their lives."

Martin, who in December 2011 was appointed as a consulter to the Vatican Council for the New Evangelization, predicts that by 2022 FOCUS will have graduated 75,000 practicing Catholics from college campuses in the United States. "That's 75,000 people who pray, believe in evangelization and are committed to serving God and others for the rest of their lives. That's enough to put four committed young Catholics in every parish in America."

He cites Dom Jean-Baptiste Chautard, who in the book *The Soul of the Apostolate*, said that one faithful priest surrounded by three Catholics who are thoroughly converted and committed to mission can transform a parish. "So we're all going to play a role in revolutionizing the Catholic Church's experience of itself, of Catholics' experience of the Catholic faith within the next ten years."

What will that "revolution" look like? Martin says the culture has convinced most Catholics that their faith must be so private that there's been a general amnesia about what the Church's deepest identity entails: evangelization. The Church exists to bring the Good News to others.

"Once we reintroduce people to their deepest identity, when they realize they're supposed to be evangelistic—it's a good thing to share good news—they come alive in their faith."

*John Burger is a freelance writer and editor based in Connecticut.*

CHAPTER TWO

# Light for the East— The New Evangelization in Eastern Europe

*Emily Stimpson*

E**VIL HAS A WAY OF** lingering. That's a truth Catholics in the East know all too well.

On November 9, 1989, the Berlin Wall fell. Two years later, on December 26, 1991, the Soviet Union itself broke apart. At the time, Communism's long reign across Eastern Europe seemed to be at an end. And it was…up to a point.

In some countries, market economies and free political systems soon emerged. In others, Communist leaders remained in power, with only the names of their parties changed. And in the two decades since, other countries still have witnessed the ebb and flow of Communists losing power, then regaining it once more.

It isn't, however, simply in the governments of the East that Communism has lingered. It also has lingered in the culture, in the people, in the way they live their lives and see the world. It especially has lingered in the way they live their faith. Or in many cases, the way they don't.

There is no simple way of summing up what was done to Catholics in the East during the reign of Soviet Communism. In some places and times the Church was completely suppressed, with parishes, schools, and seminaries shuttered, priests killed or sent into exile, and all expressions of the faith banned from public life. In other places and times, the Church was used as an arm of the state or permitted to exist in only the most rudimentary of forms; Masses could be offered, but no formation outside the Mass could be given.

Regardless, it was always and everywhere a liability—professional and social—to be a Catholic. Those who went to Mass on Sundays or had their children baptized were prohibited from attending university, teaching in schools, or advancing in their careers. Some were arrested. Others fired from their jobs.

Accordingly, in families that did persist in the faith, parents forbade their children to tell their classmates that they were Catholic. Some, not trusting their children to keep such a secret, never informed them of their baptism until they were grown. Friends didn't talk about their faith with one another, let alone share it, and formation in the Christian virtues became all but impossible in the midst of a society where lying, cheating, and bribing were essential to surviving.

Over time, a culture of silence and secrecy about the faith took root. Thanks to those within the Church who cooperated with the Communist governments, so too did a culture of mistrust. The sins of her children compromised the Church's credibility, undermining her ability to speak to the moral, political, and theological challenges of the time.

That was true in 1989 when the Berlin Wall fell, and, it's still largely true today. Even where belief in Christ and his Church runs deep, it remains unusual for people to talk with others about matters of faith. Communism drew a sharp line between what happens inside the church on Sunday and what occurs every other day of the week. In many places that line has never been erased, making the integration of private faith and public life difficult for some—unheard of for others.

At the same time, mounting challenges from the West such as consumerism, hedonism, and secularism, have continued to flood Eastern Europe in recent years, numbing in many quarters the interest shown in the faith in the first years of freedom. Twenty-five years ago it was the Communists telling Catholics they couldn't speak about their faith without suffering the consequences. Today that same message is coming from the media and from the culture at large.

Yet in the midst of it all, God is still at work, and the work of the New Evangelization goes on. In the most unlikely of places, something is afoot in Eastern Europe—movements of grace rich with the promise of renewal.

## A Catholic Normandy

There is a beachhead of the New Evangelization in Eastern Europe, and it has unlikely origins—in the American Midwest. The Language and Catechetical Institute (LCI) in Gaming, Austria sits two hours southwest of Vienna, in the *Kartause Maria Thron*, a restored fourteenth-century monastery that once hosted Soviet troops. Who took the Russians' place? The Franciscan University of Steubenville, which in 1992, with the help of the United States Conference of Catholic Bishops, set up the LCI as a spinoff of its study-abroad program in Gaming. From the beginning its goal was to educate and form Catholics from the former Soviet Union and Eastern bloc, giving them the tools they needed to rebuild the Church in the East. Rev. Michael Scanlon, TOR, then president of Franciscan University, called the program a Catholic Normandy, "a beachhead for evangelization in Europe." LCI's one-year program was designed with a threefold mission:

- To give Catholics from the East, who were long denied opportunities for academic and professional

advancement, the English language skills necessary for success in a post-communist world.
- To provide young people who showed a predisposition for leadership in the Church a fundamental knowledge of the faith through catechetical instruction and the opportunity to take more advanced classes in theology as their English progressed.
- To give them an experience of what a lived faith in Catholic community was like—an experience made possible by sharing worship, dining, living, and classroom space with Franciscan University students.

The LCI currently has students from Ukraine, Russia, Slovakia, The Czech Republic, Romania, and Serbia, as well as China, who have come to study English and catechetics, free of charge. More than 400 students from some twenty-six countries have attended LCI, then returned to their home countries to jump-start Catholic missions and support parish work where help is desperately needed.

According to the program's codirector Jennifer Healy, the success of LCI's mission has hinged in large part on the quality of its students. "Because many are chosen by their bishop, we get some of the very best young people from the East," she explained. Franciscan's students have also played a vital role. LCI students room, eat, and study with these Americans, whose presence makes it possible to have both total immersion in the English language and in Catholic life. Healy explains, "The LCI students come to us with an ingrained fear of talking about their faith. Franciscan students, however, are just the opposite. They love talking about Jesus and the Church, and they love expressing the commitment they've made to God in so many ways. Seeing that has a huge impact on the LCI students." Throw in solid teaching in the basics of the *Catechism of the Catholic Church*, opportunities to travel to Rome, Assisi, and pilgrimage sites throughout Central Europe, plus a daily routine shaped by the Church's liturgy—the Morning Office, noon Mass, evening prayer, and adoration—and you have what Healy called "the perfect storm for conversion."

To understand LCI's mission, let's look at just a few stories of students who have attended, and the challenges they face in living and spreading the Gospel.

## A Crisis of Faith and Virtue

Artur Bubnevich is tired. His long, lean body bounds energetically through the corridors of the Uzhhorod cathedral offices, but the lines on his face—too many lines for someone only thirty-six years old—betray the underlying exhaustion.

Bubnevich has reason to be exhausted. Over the past six years, as special projects coordinator for the Byzantine Catholic eparchy of Mukachevo in western Ukraine, he has singlehandedly overseen the construction of nearly

160 parishes and 25 parish houses. Plans for 40 more parishes and 160 parish houses are in the works.

Right now, however, Bubnevich's main concern is the restoration of the eparchy's sprawling eighteenth-century bishop's residence and office complex here in Uzhhorod. The complex, like everything else the Ruthenian Greek Catholic Church in Mukachevo once owned—parishes, houses, schools, seminaries, and orphanages—was taken from the Church in 1947, two years after the Soviet Union excised the Transcarpathian region from Czechoslovakia and declared it part of Ukraine.

When the Soviets arrived, they immediately ordered the bishops, priests, and people to convert to Orthodoxy, declaring all Eastern-rite Catholics "traitors to the state." Under the leadership of Bishop Theodore Romzha, the Catholics of Mukachevo at first resisted. Most, however, only held out for as long as Bishop Romzha lived. Once he was dead—at the hands of the Soviet secret police—and 120 more priests were killed or exiled, all of the eparchy's property was confiscated, and the remaining faithful moved underground.

For the next forty-five years, the Ruthenian Catholics who held fast to the faith worshipped in secret, usually at night and always with sentinels posted, on the lookout for spies and raiding parties. Priests were few and the Divine Liturgy rare. As time passed, the underground could not reach the entire population, and in many families, children grew up to be "good communists."

Independence arrived in late 1991, but save for the cathedral and fewer than a third of the churches, none of the stolen properties in Mukachevo were returned.

That's where Bubnevich comes in. It is his job to make up for all that the Byzantine Catholic Church in his eparchy lost fifty-five years ago. For the past six years, he has worked day and night carrying out the ambitious rebuilding plan put into place by Bishop Milan Shashik at the beginning of his tenure in Mukachevo.

Bubnevich, like most Ukranians his age, was baptized secretly as a baby but raised as an atheist. "Growing up, I was just a normal kid in the Soviet Union," he explained. "I was a Young Pioneer and did all the normal stuff Soviet kids did. I believed it all, about Lenin and the Communist party. But it turned out to be a big lie. That left me—left many—with a deep wound. When you finally realized the truth, you felt cheated."

It was curiosity, more than anything else, that led Bubnevich to go to Divine Liturgy once it became possible to attend. At the time, the novelty of religion attracted many people, young and old. For Bubnevich, however, it quickly became something more.

"I was one of those people for whom religion was a totally new discovery," he recalled. "I lived in a system where there was no God, then suddenly this new world opens. At first that seemed really fearful, but at some point, I saw that I only needed to say yes. As long as I said yes and wanted it, then God would lead me. And he has."

In the mid-1990s, Artur was sent by the eparchy to study English and theology in Austria. Not until his return did he begin to see the extent of Communism's legacy. "How people relate to each other, how they respect each other—you feel the difference as soon as you reach the border," he said. "For me, it was shocking."

Years later, the shock has worn off, but the problems remain. Although two decades have passed since the Soviet Union fell, much in Ukraine remains stagnant, starting with the country's economy—which remains one of the weakest of all the former Soviet states. Corruption and nepotism dominate the government.

"We have to choose between bad and worse," Bubnevich remarked about the candidates in one of the country's upcoming elections.

Smuggling and illegal trading remain a primary source of employment in this border town, while decay and neglect of buildings, roads, and homes is evident everywhere. Even many of the new buildings are falling apart. The local Ukrainian Catholic seminary was built only in 1995, but already the roof and doors need replacing, while black mold covers the dome of its chapel, completed just four years ago.

"It's like it always was," said Bubnevich about the seminary's infrastructure problems. "Cheap materials, workers who don't care; something's always wrong."

It's the lack of faith among this once deeply Catholic people, however, that concerns Bubnevich the most. "People were taught for fifty years that the family is not important, that there is no God," he said. "Three generations passed and people came to believe that. Now, so many temptations come from the West and also from the East, so people struggle to resist."

He continued, "Twenty years ago everyone wanted churches. Now we build them, and many stand empty. That is the most important point that we are trying now to repair, and this is a huge work ahead, much more than this infrastructure revival. We must make people realize that they are the ones that build the Church, and that this Church is not a building, but a body that lives."

At LCI, Bubnevich was able to spend a full year surrounded—for the first time in his life—with other Catholics who joyfully, openly talked about their faith and how to incorporate it into everyday life. "Growing up in the Soviet Union, we were taught to listen, not to think, to obey blindly, and that shaped how you thought of God, if you thought of him at all," he said. "Coming to LCI, I had very much an Old Testament understanding of God, as this strict, authoritarian figure who I should be afraid of and who would punish me if I did anything wrong. But at LCI, I saw how my teachers and their families, my fellow students, and especially the Americans, loved God. I saw how rich the Church was with love, and that showed me another way. I came to understand God as a Father, who loves me tenderly. That's what I'm trying to show the people I work with now."

## The Lure of Bling

"Missionary work used to be so much easier," said LCI graduate Dr. Laco Bučko. "Today, it requires more work, more creativity."

Bučko should know. The Slovak native has spent the better part of the past twenty years either serving as a missionary or forming them. His first foray into missionary work was in the early 1990s, shortly after he graduated from university in Bratislava with a degree in cybernetics. Unable to conceive of "a life spent always with computers," and blackballed from the seminary by the Communists who, at the time, still controlled it, Bučko decided to pursue missionary work instead. "I told my mother I would be back in three months," he recalled. "I was gone three years."

Bučko headed first to Russia. There, in the shadow of the KGB offices in Moscow, he and his fellow missionaries spent most of their time working with young people at St. Louis Parish. "People were hungry for knowledge about God, about Jesus, about the Church, and they were asking," he said, "It was very easy work. We sat in the church, opened the door, and young people just came and asked questions."

After Russia, Bučko traveled to Uzbekistan, Tajikistan, Kazakhstan, and Siberia—all with guitar in hand—evangelizing and leading prayer meetings. He then returned home for further training in theology, eventually moving his young family to Bratislava, where he joined the faculty of St. Elizabeth University and helped found the John

Paul II Institute of Missiology and Tropical Diseases. Now, as a missiology professor, he teaches young Slovaks how to do what he once did. Working in partnership with other non-profit organizations, the John Paul II Institute has ongoing projects in more than twenty countries, including Haiti, Rwanda, and Vietnam. Many of the projects are medical missions, but they also include schools, orphanages, and program for underprivileged youth.

Right now 520 students study at the Institute, which is housed on the outskirts of Bratislava in a sprawling industrial park whose design recalls politburos and central planning committees. Since its founding in 2003, 5,000 students have completed the program. Most come as baptized Catholics, but according to Bučko it's not the desire to share the faith that attracts the majority of them to the Institute.

"They're interested in doing good, in social work," he said. "Many aren't practicing their faith but they find the idea of helping others attractive. For some, as they go through the program, that changes. But not for all."

As Bučko sees it, students' lack of interest in the underlying reason for missionary work—sharing the Gospel—is a symptom of the consumerism that has swept Slovakia in the years since the Communists left power. He explained, "For me, half my life I lived under the Communist regime. The second half, I lived in the Democratic regime. And I am glad that I had the Communist experience. Yes, it was difficult, but it was good, in a way, for us to go without material things, to all wear the same clothes and use the same equipment in the household. It was good because we didn't look to material things to fill the hunger inside us. We looked to spiritual things."

"The young people today," he continued, "they have the same hunger, but they are told that it is the material things that will fill that hunger. Many believe that." It's that attitude that Bučko strives to counter among his students. "Communism, in the strangest of ways, prepared the soil for a spiritual explosion in the East," Bučko said. "There's so much hunger. It would be ideal if we could find a way to merge the freedom of the West with this hunger for spirituality in the East."

"I had so many prejudices when I came to LCI," recalled Laco Bučko. "Especially about the Americans. But living together, you come to see people so differently. You see their faith, you see different ways of approaching problems, and thinking about the world. It changes everything."

## What to Learn from the West?

In Hungary, as elsewhere in Europe, the Christian faith is in decline. "Twenty years ago when you went to Mass, the churches were full," observed a diplomat for the Hungarian government (and LCI grad) who spoke to me when I visited. "Now, with few exceptions, they're half-empty. We are looking for friends, and we try to find friends, but there are only small groups to find. Catholics make up in a diaspora in Europe." Although six million of the country's ten million people are Catholic, only 20 percent of the baptized go to Church at least occasionally, and only 10 percent—one million out of ten million—go regularly.

Those numbers both reflect and are a result of the mounting secularism in a country that, in spite of its current center-right ruling coalition, has struggled more than most to rid its government of Socialists and former Communists. "Before 1989, you could never talk about faith," said LCI alumnus Csaba Szabo, a lawyer who works with American firms operating overseas. "Then, for a short while, we had a time where we could, where we were free. Now freedom has brought the pro-choice culture."

Although the current hostility toward the faith comes from that culture, not the government, the Hungarian Catholics gathered for lunch still feel the hostility acutely. Many struggle to find Catholic community. Others are at a loss as to how to live their faith in their profession or make the case for belief in the public square.

"Ten years ago, I wasn't even familiar with the terms 'pro-life' and 'pro-choice,'" added Szabo. "Now, suddenly, our society has reached the point that when you say you are against abortion, you are dismissed as old-fashioned. We have to learn a new way of talking about these things. And we have to teach our children a new way of talking about these things."

At LCI Szabo learned some of the new, effective means of defending the culture of life that have emerged in the American prolife movement. "Americans have the resources, and they have the experience," he explained. "They know they have to be clever. We have to learn to be clever too so we can influence people in a positive way. We're trying, but you look at how Americans do it and how we do it, and we're not there yet."

## Reweaving the Fabric

Some of LCI's students are new converts, such as Yuliya Ermakovich, a twenty-four-year-old sociologist who worked at the Moscow Institute of Cultural and Social Programs before coming to LCI. Baptized Orthodox, but raised with no religion, Yuliya's first encounter with the Church came when she was sixteen. A school field trip took her to the Moscow cathedral. That was all she needed. "As soon as I walked in, I felt for the first time that God was near my heart," she recalled. Yuliya came to LCI at the recommendation of the mother superior of the order she's considering joining.

Then there are cradle Catholics like Barbara Ninacs, a nineteen-year-old from Romania, who has thus far managed to escape the destructive influences of extreme poverty and a crime-ridden community primarily because of her love for the Church. "Until I was in seventh grade, I never took my faith seriously," Ninacs explains. "Then a new priest came to our parish who reached out to the young people. That changed everything. I began to discover what it meant to be a Catholic and to live that out in a holy way." In high school, Ninacs worked with her parish to set up youth camps and programs for young children. Her goal is to run an apostolate that ministers to children with special needs, whom she says are among the most neglected people in Romania.

Other LCI students include Valentina Khaimyk, from Ukraine, who grew up in a village where the the nearest parish was an hour's walk away; Mariya Yuzupanova, from Kazakhstan, a country where only 1.5 percent of the population is Catholic; Gratiela Labud, whose grandfather, a Greek Catholic priest, died for the Catholic faith under Communism; Krstyna Hronova, who grew up in a family with twelve children, something unheard of in Western and Eastern Europe today; and Srdjan Muharem, a Catholic from the Orthodox dominated country of Serbia who wants to become a theology professor.

Each has come to LCI for a different reason—some to learn English, some for the theology, some because a parish priest or relative thought the program their best chance to escape the encroaching secularism in the East. All, however, say they have known the loneliness that comes from being a young, practicing Catholic in Eastern Europe today.

"To see the American students and to be with other students from Europe who believe their faith, who practice it and live it, it's like being in an entirely different universe," explained Ninacs. "They embrace this Catholic life and cherish it. I really didn't know such people existed."

That is exactly why LCI does exist: Not only to show those raised in the shadow of communism that a different way of life is possible, but to show them what that life looks like, to teach them how to live it, and to equip them to teach others how to live it as well. Graduates of LCI have gone on to enter the priesthood and religious life, to found marriage preparation programs and Bible studies, to restore churches and monasteries, staff diocesan chancery offices, lead youth groups, and take on many other vital tasks entailed in re-evangelizing the lands where atheism was long imposed by force—and faith must now be found in freedom.

## An Integrated Christian Life

Perhaps if the secret to LCI's success had to be summed up in one word, it would be "integration"—the integration of East and West, English and catechesis, prayer and study, faith, and life. In the *Kartause*, all is woven together into one seamless experience of Catholic life. In the midst of that life, prejudices are broken down, hearts opened, friendships made, virtue acquired, and faith formed. In the midst of that life, true conversion takes place.

Lessons like that, however, aren't learned in the abstract. They are learned in the concrete and the personal, in the daily rhythm of study and worship and in the relationships that are fostered between students from vastly different backgrounds.

"At LCI I met people who were open to sharing the faith and talking and praying together," said Helena

Ivorikova, who graduated from LCI in 1998 and now hosts a talk show for Slovakia's first Catholic television station. "This helped me very much, and I too started to be open. Growing up, this being open was forbidden. We never talked about the faith, we never discussed it. But at LCI it was just part of everyday life. We study, we eat, we go to Mass and adoration, and it just became normal."

"Eucharistic adoration was something I really did not understand when I arrived. I would watch these students go and sit in the chapel for an hour or two and it seemed so strange. But they would invite me to go too, and I did, and eventually, I understood. Now I cannot get enough of this great experience of love," Ivorikova said.

LCI's greatest gift to its students is that personal experience of conversion. It helps light or fan the flame of faith in the young people who come to study there, giving them both the desire and the tools they need to be effective disciples of the New Evangelization.

And LCI's graduates are eager to take on that task, for the benefit of their friends and family back home. "You can still find people who have faith in Russia, but they haven't enough knowledge of it," Yuliya Ermakovich explained. "It's the history of our country. It's Communism. It's taken away the Christian traditions and left us with different ideas, different teachers and opinions, a different way of life. So, even if you have faith, it can be easily lost." But Ermakovich is full of hope. "Our history is like a magic story, a fairy tale, that has not ended yet. We as a Church need to give them what others cannot."

*Emily Stimpson is an award-winning Catholic writer based in Steubenville, Ohio. She is the author of* The Catholic Girl's Survival Guide for the Single Years, *a contributing editor to* Our Sunday Visitor, *and a frequent contributor to* Franciscan Way, The National Catholic Register, Lay Witness, Catholic Vote, *and many other publications. This chapter is a revision and expansion of a piece that appeared in* Our Sunday Visitor *on November 9, 2012.*

## CHAPTER THREE

# Mother Angelica and the Founding of EWTN

### *Deirdre Folley*

For any American under the age of forty or so, the Eternal Word Television Network has seemed like a force or a monument of nature—a twenty-four-hour TV source for news, religious education, commentary, and more, as well as a radio and Internet location for all matters Catholic. This solid, go-to source for reliable, faithfully Catholic commentary has become such a fact of life that it's easy to forget that it hasn't always just "been there"—that before its founding in 1981, religious TV was almost entirely dominated by evangelical Protestants, with a smattering of sentimental, social-justice programming crafted by Catholics, and the occasional Sunday Mass broadcast at six a.m. on a local station.

EWTN may feel to us like the Grand Canyon, but in fact it is really much more like Mount Rushmore—the fruit of astonishing labor by a single dedicated person whose vision overcame a dizzying array of obstacles. The full picture comes to light in Raymond Arroyo's definitive biography, *Mother Angelica: The Remarkable Story of a Nun, Her Nerve, and a Network of Miracles*.[1]

To become familiar with Mother Angelica, the woman behind EWTN, is to become familiar with an indomitable spirit, a history of miracles, and a series of successes that are impossible *not* to attribute to divine intervention. It may be difficult to reconcile the enormous personality of Mother Angelica, revealed in Arroyo's biography, with the gentle, grandmotherly, calm presence on the TV screen. Yet this is the secret of the birth and success of EWTN and the movement of Catholic communications. God sometimes uses surprising instruments for his purposes.

## The Unlikely Entrepreneur

Born Rita Rizzo, the girl who would become the most important figure in American Catholic broadcasting was a misfit in an Italian community located in a crime-ridden part of an Ohio town. Her mother, Mae Rizzo, was always unstable but became more so after divorcing her abusive husband John. The rift left a stigma on Mae and her daughter: they were the only family in the parish to have experienced divorce. As a youth in the Great Depression, Rita could not depend on either parent for care and had no secure source of moral formation. "I used to wonder if there was a God," Angelica recalls, "and if there was such a person I couldn't figure out why He wouldn't let me have a family, like the other kids."[2] With her disadvantaged background and no foundation for her faith, the odds were against Rita's success in high school—to say nothing of the possibility that she would become one of the most powerful women in the Church.

But after receiving a miraculous healing as a young woman, Rita fell in love with God. She responded to a call to leave her broken family and broken town in search for the peace of a cloister. Having found a home and a stable family among the sisters in religious life, the once withdrawn youth proved to be a natural leader and drew upon her rough childhood for inspiration. On one occasion, in order to finance a new grotto on the monastery grounds—and hoping to do some missionary work at the same time—Angelica called upon an old connection she had from Canton, Ohio, whom she knew to be an important figure in organized crime. She convinced him to gather donations on behalf of Our Lady from "all the boys" so that their names could be written down on parchment and buried in the statue. "Nobody's going to see it," she told the boss, "it'll be buried in concrete, like you're going to be one of these days if you don't straighten up" (83).

Within the first year after taking her final vows, Sister Angelica already began considering establishing a new community. While praying from a hospital bed, where she was awaiting a risky surgery that might result in her being unable to walk again, she bargained with God that if she were healed, she would go and begin a special ministry to African-Americans struggling in the segregation-ridden state of Alabama. About five years later, in 1961, having raised funds by handcrafting and selling fishing lures—which she sold to local Protestants at baseball games, naming them for St. Peter—she was on her way to fulfill her mission. It would take a very different form than she had imagined.

Having arrived in the South, Angelica's first project was to build and to get her community settled. The physically feeble nun, for whom building of any kind was a new enterprise, took on the role of overseer of construction for the monastery, effectively managing the various teams on the job and addressing problems as they arose. When a problematic cavern was found in the middle of her site, she simply stated, "We'll find a hill around here somewhere and just put it in there" (98). Sure enough, not long thereafter, a man came upon the scene and proffered, "I got a hill in back a' my house. . . . You want it?" The dirt was provided and work went forward, according to her plan (93).

Once settled, Angelica's mission rapidly evolved according to the needs she observed. She agreed to lead a weekly Scripture study with a group of women of various Christian faiths who were drawn to her strong spiritual presence. As the one original study group grew to include several by 1971, and the demand for Angelica's teaching increased, she began recording talks on cassette and eventually was booked for a regular radio program. Despite her meager education, she went on to write booklets and then books on Catholic teaching and spirituality. At the same time she found funding for a 1973 bumper-sticker campaign against the "mind pollution" of pornography. In 1975, when her regular printer fell through, she took the plunge to set up an in-house printing press. While she kept up these various ways of teaching with prolific output, she also traveled around the country giving talks, supporting the monastery with her speaking fees.

One trip to Chicago in 1978 sparked Angelica's imagination: she encountered Baptist-run Channel 38 and was struck with the possibility of sharing the Gospel over the airwaves. Shortly thereafter she had a deal for a regular show, and the woman who had rarely laid eyes on a TV set was quickly recognized as a natural in front of the camera. But when her network's affiliate aired a blasphemous show, Angelica knew she needed her own, independent broadcasting outlet. So in 1979, without any experience or resources, she moved forward with plans to set up a studio in the monastery garage. Two years later EWTN was officially founded. By this time, the woman who was once floundering and lonely was becoming a powerful voice with a strong following and devoted supporters, poised to spring onto a national and then global theater.

Angelica could tackle all these daunting tasks because while she was ahead of her times in many ways, in others she was very much a woman of the times. Her desire to live in the moment enabled her to be very flexible—never on principles, but always in practice and in responsiveness to the Holy Spirit. Angelica lived out what she taught—"that we see his Providence in the present moment"[3]—in all her activities. "I think the best preparation is to have no preparation," she wrote of her experiences in public speaking in 1961, "Jesus will tell me what to say when the time comes" (95).

As much as she lived in the moment and adapted to the times, however, there was one constant in Angelica's life as a religious: devoted friendship with God and adoration of Jesus in the Eucharist. Her frequently changed, but always due to promptings she found in prayer and meditation. Her work was always supported by the fervent prayers of her community and peppered with miracles that showed God's favor for her choices.

## Against the Bureaucrats

Time and again, leading up to the founding of EWTN and at numerous occasions thereafter, Angelica found herself in conflict with the American bishops, in a series of clashes that ranged in severity from mild disagreement to protracted canonical battle. For someone acquainted only with the slow-talking, gentle spiritual adviser who appeared on television screens in episodes of *Mother Angelica Live*, it might seem improbable that this woman could ever have been in conflict with the stewards of the American Church. But the chronicle of her disagreements with the hierarchy reveals some troubling weaknesses in the episcopal leadership of the American Church—as well as the indomitable spirit of a nun who would not back away from her princples.

Angelica had her first experience of disagreeing with a bishop when she felt called to start a community in the South. Bishop Emmet Michael Walsh of Youngstown, Ohio (where her monastery was located) objected, fearing that her existing community could not withstand the departure of a group of its members. Although his objection was a fair one, Angelica chipped away at it with a persuasive letter accompanied by committed prayer, and he eventually relented. While she respected his authority, she did not hesitate to share her side of the matter, including her resolute determination to do what she believed the Spirit called her to do.

Writing a letter to plead her cause with Bishop Walsh of Ohio was only a mild indication of Angelica's determination, however. Consequent clashes were enough to put enormous strains both on EWTN and on the entire episcipal conference (which at the time was known as the National Conference of Catholic Bishops, or NCCB). Even at the height of the rising influence of EWTN, the

NCCB was by no means convinced that Mother Angelica was the right person to hold so much sway over Catholic preaching and teaching through the media. The bishops had decided to launch their own Catholic television channel, the Catholic Telecommunications Network of American (CTNA), and did not appreciate the competition.

On one hand it is understandable that the bishops would worry that a single nun, surrounded by a small group of lay workers and advisors, should wield control over such a powerful means of reaching the American faithful. However, if the bishops had really been concerned primarily about orthodoxy in teaching, they should have been able to reach some amicable agreement with a woman who had, thus far in her project, shown herself entirely faithful to Catholic teaching and committed to prayer and sacrifice. Instead the NCCB worked to edge EWTN out of the game.

Since there was a limited amount of space on the airwaves for Catholic television, and local cable broadcasters were reluctant to carry two different Catholic networks, CTNA provided the greatest threat to the survival of EWTN, at precisely the time that EWTN was establishing itself as an American broadcasting superpower. But Mother Angelica was not interested in yielding any hard-won ground to the NCCB. She fought to save her independent network—in large part, ironically, because she did not trust the bishops to carry out the authentic evangelizing mission of the Church, at a time when some

American bishops and their staff members were openly distancing themselves from the Pope and questioning traditional Catholic teachings. Ultimately, despite its comparative lack of material resources, EWTN and its faithful founder won the contest with the bishops' well-funded project. Raymond Arroyo recalls:

> Many bishops interviewed blamed CTNA's overly broad programming for its failure and eventual demise. As early as 1983, Catholics in Rhode Island and elsewhere began protesting CTNA's programming, convinced it presented a mix of "modernism and liberal politics" injurious to their faith. The program *Spirituality in the Eighties*, a series of interviews with dissenting theologians Hans Küng, Edward Schillebeeckx, and others explaining their "faith experience" was mentioned by name.... One bishop, speaking on the condition of anonymity, said, "Nobody could watch it.... The bureaucrats were running that thing, not the conference." (209)

The decision that allowed EWTN to move forward without further threats from CTNA was made in a gathering of the bishops' conference that involved a secret vote and negotiations with the surprisingly powerful nun. When one bishop asked whether the crucial vote could figuratively "kill Mother Angelica," Bishop Anthony Bosco was quoted as saying, "I don't think anyone could kill Mother Angelica—not if you know her. She won't let anyone kill her" (214). There was certainly some tension among the parties involved, since by this time Angelica had made it clear that she did not regard all the bishops as faithful teachers in line with the magisterium. Once it was clear that Mother Angelica held the upper hand, the bishops had to angle for some role in her network.

Before retiring from public life, Angelica would be involved in several other disputes with Church leaders, including Princes of the Church. She challenged Cardinal Bernard Law of Boston about the inclusive-language English edition of the *Catechism of the Catholic Church* that he had commissioned. (She won that argument; the Vatican called for a thorough revision of the translation.) She had a bitter feud with Cardinal Roger Mahony of Los Angeles over the Church's teaching on the Eucharist, after Mother Angelica boldly criticized Mahoney on her live show for echoing Lutheran doctrine in his pastoral writing. While she would ultimately show deference to decisions coming from Rome and her beloved Pope John Paul II, she had very little patience with his intermediaries on American soil. Although she sometimes found herself in very troubled waters because of her sharp tongue and unapologetic stance, she may also have been a lifeline for Church leaders in America, in ways that will only be clear in the long run.

## The Theology of Risk

What made EWTN work? What was the secret behind this uneducated woman, with no background in media, who started out with nothing, and eventually established a Catholic media empire against the expectations of the world and even the wishes of many Church authorities? The paradox of Mother Angelica's approach is that she never had a plan and refused to make a plan. She simply relied on God and, like a demanding wife, allowed him to show his love by taking every advantage of his kindness.

Mother Angelica is a woman of miracles, so it is fitting that her great work, EWTN, is built upon miracles. When she was a child, she was rescued from an oncoming bus by inexplicably being lifted off of the ground and carried to safety by an invisible presence. As a sick twenty-year-old with a hopeless case of a displaced stomach, she received a truly miraculous healing through the intercession of a local mystic, Rhoda Wise who had herself experienced the stigmata and other sufferings of Christ. As a young nun preparing for vows, Angelica's vocation seemed in jeopardy when kneeling became impossible due to painful swelling of the knees. But when she made her plan to begin a community in the South, not only did her knees improve, but doctors told her that a warmer climate would promote full healing.

Angelica received similar personal gifts throughout her life and the founding of EWTN, with the climactic event occurring in her old age. After being confined to cumbersome leg braces and a walker, she encountered another mystic, Paola Albertini, whose intercessory prayer straightened out her joints, returned muscle tone to her legs, and restored to her the independence of a considerably more vigorous physique. Mother Angelica learned a great deal through her experiences about the value of suffering, but she also learned to expect and receive great and amazing things from God.

Perhaps because she personally experienced the power of God's intervention in everyday events, she stunned everyone around her with her reliance on his will, even to the point of apparent folly. She shunned both strategy and planning, convinced that employing them would only shortchange the superior plans God had in store. Repeatedly, with every step of her adventures in executing a mission, she would sign on to a project before having any idea of how she would finance it.

At times in the establishment and upkeep of EWTN, Mother Angelica went into outrageous debt, buoyed by the simple conviction that the money would come through at the appropriate time. The expenses that accompany work in the television business are immense—studio equipment, crew, satellite access, cable deals, etc.—but to her these were not real obstacles. "We never know where the next penny's coming from. That's what I'm trying to get through people's heads: This is an act of God" (191). On one notable occasion, when she was under pressure from officials in Rome and local bishops to curtail her evangelizing activity, a satellite dish she had ordered was due for delivery. To her dismay, she found that the dish could not be unloaded until she made a payment of $600,000. Excusing herself to the chapel, she abandoned the case into the hands of God. She promptly received a phone call from a friend informing Angelica that a donor had just been moved to contribute $600,000 to her work, and that yes, he could wire the money to her immediately.

Following what appeared to be similarly reckless decisions, Angelica rushed headlong into her radio project, which would cost a stunning twenty-three million dollars in startup costs. The radio project was an assignment from God, she believed, which she had received during prayer. Later in life she moved just as quickly to build her monastery in Hanceville, the fruit of a similar abrupt inspiration. While visiting Bogota, Columbia, on a trip related to EWTN business, she received instructions from the Child Jesus to build a shrine; and at the age of seventy-two, she began what would eventually be Our Lady of the Angels Monastery and the Shrine of the Most Blessed Sacrament. Providentially, with each new idea, donors came through and friends picked up the tab. "Money is his problem," she once declared. "Working for the Kingdom is mine" (129).

"Faith is one foot on the ground, one foot in the air, and a queasy feeling in the stomach," she said (153). While some might have a queasy feeling merely thinking about the risks she took and the quantities of money she spent, this was the only way Mother Angelica could run operations. In the end she defied the doubters.

## The Ridiculous and the Miraculous

Today EWTN's reach is global. Its affiliates in radio, online news, and television abound. Its programming includes outreach for children, podcasts, and mobile streaming video. It has reached millions upon millions of people all around the world, thanks to the tenacity and outrageous faith of one unlikely woman.

In the United States, Mother Angelica and EWTN are among the primary influences that have kept Catholic traditions alive through the very turbulent time of the second half of the twentieth-century and into the new millennium. Angelica's devotion to all her missions, and in particular her very public devotion to the Real Presence, has been a challenge to Americans when many have lost faith in the Eucharist. Her televised ministry of belief in providence and miracles has inspired many who were disillusioned and tempted to capitulate to the powers of a culture of death. The live broadcasts of papal activities and travels on EWTN are almost certainly a large factor in the renewal of devotion and obedience to the papacy, particularly in a younger generation of Catholics. Even her controversial relationship with the American bishops has helped expose structural problems within the bishops conference that weakened their leadership of the Church. In the realm of American religious life, Mother Angelica's nuns are an example of traditional piety and practice to the American public, even while many other orders have cast off their obedience to Church teaching along with their habits. Even the telecast Mass of Angelica's community has been influential for the American Church; Bishop David Foley of Birmingham attributes the widespread use of the traditional *Kyrie* and *Agnus Dei* to the example set by EWTN (231).

Bishop Foley who also stated, "Who founded the New Evangelization in the United States? Mother Angelica did" (329). Whether or not Angelica is a household name among today's American Catholics, and whether or not the American Church is flourishing yet, Catholics in the United States would be considerably worse off had the brave Angelica not repeatedly answered the call to evangelize with her whole heart.

In his biography of Angelica, Arroyo quotes her book *The Keys to the Kingdom:* "We use the talents we possess to the best of our ability and leave the results to God. We are at peace in the knowledge that he is pleased with our efforts and that his providence will take care of the fruit of those efforts" (127). Catholics in America, and all around the world, who strive and pray for a renewal of faith and the spreading of the Kingdom on earth, can be grateful to God for generously blessing the fruits of the efforts of his servant Angelica, who used her talents so zealously in pursuit of souls.

Mother Angelica once said: "Unless you are willing to do the ridiculous, God will not do the miraculous" (146). Her work and its unlikely success is an inspiration to any Catholic who is faced with making decisions that the world might consider "ridiculous" in order to follow God's will.

*Deirdre M. Folley is a freelance writer and research analyst living in Maryland. She blogs at Like Mother Like Daughter.*

CHAPTER FOUR

# Latin Americans Give Jesus for Christmas

## By Angelique Ruhi-López

MANY CHRISTIANS LAMENT THE over-commercialization of Christmas. A group in Peru is doing something about it by bringing Jesus back into Christmas celebrations and bringing people celebrating Christmas back to Christ.

The program is called *Navidad es Jesús*, (Christmas is Jesus), an annual campaign designed to bring hope and joy to children in need, through a visit by volunteers who play games, teach catechism, and bring gifts to the children during Advent. The campaign was created in Peru in 1985 and is organized by Movimiento de Vida Cristiana (Christian Life Movement: www.m-v-c.org), an international lay Catholic movement approved by the Holy See.

While the largest program by far exists in Peru, *Navidad es Jesús* can also be found in Costa Rica, Angola, Brazil, Ecuador, Colombia, and the Philippines.

*Navidad es Jesús* seeks to evangelize about the true meaning of Christmas: the celebration of Jesus' birth, who became man for all to be reconciled to God.

## The Nativity of Christmas

In 1985, members of the newly formed Movimiento de Vida Cristiana (MVC), were looking for a new way to integrate their faith and apostolic life. As their primary document, *"Movimiento de Vida Cristiana: ¿Qué es?"* states: "At the center of their faith experience is the desire to live for sainthood, an ardent commitment to apostleship and fraternal and generous giving of oneself in service. These three dimensions express the identity, way of life and scope of MVC."

The group, which at the time was comprised primarily of university students, was already earnestly trying to spread the word about the true meaning of the holiday by singing Christmas carols at the busy Miraflores Park in Lima. This idea evolved as members also realized that it was important to go beyond offering inspiration to something more tangible: material help to the needy, and catechesis to the ignorant. The idea grew from what MVC called a "solidarity campaign" to one that also included evangelization, as more and more people outside of the group started to join with members to spread Christmas joy, rooted in Christ.

The original name of the campaign was *"No Hay Navidad Sin Jesús"* (*"There is No Christmas Without Jesus"*) but the name was changed shortly thereafter to the more upbeat *"Navidad es Jesús."* With the change in name seemed to come positive changes in people's lives. Francisco Cañola, general coordinator of MVC in Peru, explained that at this point, those involved had a great desire to share the ministry with others; parents, siblings and friends began to get involved. "They started to knock on our door," said Cañola of the people who wanted to volunteer. "They also started to make changes in their lives, such as putting a nativity scene on their desks at work." He added: "All this shows a sense of lived experience, and an identity found in Jesus. It's great for us to help others, but let's take advantage and live this message of Christmas in our own lives as well. Charity in and of itself is very valuable but we didn't want it to be just about giving a gift to a poor child. We knew that it needed to help both the beneficiary and the benefactor."

### Bread and Milk and More

In the Lima and neighboring Callao provinces in Peru alone, volunteers bring Christmas cheer to more than 100,000 children during about 200 yearly Christmas visits. There are an estimated 12,000 volunteers who participate annually, not counting those who help behind the scenes.

During a typical Christmas visit, volunteers gather with local children in public facilities, such as schools, to play games and offer gifts. The volunteers might participate in a variety of lighthearted activities to interact with the children, then put on a play explaining the true meaning of Christmas, and distribute traditional Christmas treats of *panettone* (sweet bread) and chocolate milk, as well as individual gifts for every child. Occasional variations on the visits include separate catechesis for the parents during the children's activities, creating a nativity scene for each child to take home, or singing "happy birthday" to baby Jesus. Other visits have been to nursing homes, to offer the elderly Christmas cheer.

The program varies somewhat in Ecuador, where MVC has run *Navidad es Jesús* campaigns since 1998. There about 2,500 volunteers serve 15,000 families (about 57,000 people total) throughout many of the country's rural and marginalized areas to deliver what they call "solidarity baskets" containing rice, sugar, oil, salt, powdered milk, noodles, tuna, chocolate, oatmeal, beans, Christmas bread, and sweets.

Beginning in August of each year, MVC members involved in *Solidaridad en Marcha* (MVC's yearlong social service arm in Peru: www.solidaridadenmarcha.org), begin to identify families and areas that would most benefit from a *Navidad es Jesús* visit. Their link to the *Solidaridad en Marcha* network is mutually beneficial: *Solidaridad en Marcha* helps to identify locales and neighborhoods for *Navidad es Jesús* to schedule visits, while those who participate in *Navidad es Jesús* can then choose to help people in these areas all through the year with *Solidaridad en Marcha*. The latter campaign strives to provide for the people's basic needs, and to provide occasions for evangelization outside the Christmas season.

The typical ratio of children to volunteers is five to one, so in a visit with 100 volunteers (an average number), 500 neighborhood children might be selected for a specific *Navidad es Jesús* visit. Advance planning helps to ensure a successful visit. Beforehand, volunteers for each visit are broken up into different teams, which handle:

- infrastructure/logistics (further broken down into transportation, materials and security)
- secretarial work (organizing names and ages of children, breaking them up into groups, coordinating volunteers, etc.)
- apostolate (catechesis of both children and volunteers, children's activities, etc.)
- gifts (refreshments, toys)
- finances (donations, fundraising, purchasing).

Each of these teams is assigned tasks to be performed before, during, and after each visit. They are all overseen by a site coordinator.

Cañola makes the interesting observation that in Latin America people don't wait to be trained—or "capacitated" as he puts it—in order to begin work in a ministry. They just jump right in. The level of formation of the volunteers varies, but this does not stop them from wanting to be involved.

So MVC provides the volunteers in-depth manuals detailing what a *Navidad es Jesús* visit entails from start to finish. This allows even non-MVC members to take part in multiple visits in multiple areas. There is one general manual of logistics (which, among other important details, includes an organized schedule of events to take the guesswork out of planning all the required aspects of a Christmas visit), one for activities and catechesis, one for visual identity (which includes acceptable logos used for consistent branding of all materials and promotional items), and even a appendix of catechetical materials that includes approved handouts, coloring pages, and similar items.

The only requisite for volunteers wanting to plan their own MVC visit is that at least one MVC member with experience in the *Navidad es Jesús* program accompanies them on their first visit. The following year, non-members may do visits on their own utilizing the manuals, which include easy-to-read organizational charts and flow charts of responsibilities, as well as maps and diagrams that suggest exact staging and set-up of the main hall, offering different alternatives that depend on the site where the visit is held. These detailed workbooks help make sure that the visits retain their Catholic identity and catechetical purpose, and do not degenerate into merely social or social service events.

## Christmas Starts with Original Sin

At every Christmas visit, leaders will say many times throughout the day, *"Navidad es...."* to which the children learn to respond, *"¡Jesús!"* This is how the catechesis begins at its most basic level. "We help about 120,000 children each year. But we don't focus on the number, we focus on the message. The focus is on catechesis," said Cañola. The visit starts with a number of icebreakers (with instructions detailed in the manual), some with religious significance, such as a Christmas quiz, or others just to warm up the kids, including games akin to Simon Says.

As the day progresses, the teachings go deeper and deeper into the incarnation and Christ's birth, while still keeping the tone interesting and light-hearted for the children. A puppet show or living Nativity scene on the real meaning of Christmas (four different sample scripts are included in the manual) are at the heart of the catechetical teachings. The manual also includes criteria for catechesis, which insist that the following points be made:

- Adam and Eve misbehaved and disobeyed God. God was very sad but he did not abandon us.
- God is so good that he wanted to forgive us and to do so, he sent us his son, Jesus.

- Jesus is the son of God, who is born of the Virgin Mary.
- The angel Gabriel came down from heaven and asked Mary if she wanted to be Jesus' mother.
- She accepted and asked what she could do.
- The Holy Spirit came down from heaven and placed baby Jesus inside Mary's womb.
- Joseph was Mary's husband and at first, he didn't know what to do.
- The angel Gabriel appeared to Joseph in his dreams and told him that what Mary said was true.
- Joseph accepted Jesus and loved him very much.
- One day, Mary and Joseph had to travel to Bethlehem to be counted in the census and they could not find a place to stay, so Mary had to give birth to Jesus in a stable.
- The shepherds and the three wise men came to visit Jesus, guided by a star.

After the puppet show or skit, the volunteers engage the children in dialogue about what they saw and heard. They ask questions and invite the children to say a prayer, sing Jesus a song, or give Jesus a gift in their hearts in honor of his birth. The children are then broken up into groups by age (four- to five-year-olds; eight- to nine-year-olds; and ten years and up) and are given a variety of coloring pages or age-appropriate activities to drive home the message of Christmas. The volunteers also lead the children in singing Christmas carols and in numerous prayers, including opening and closing prayers, a prayer before eating their snack, and a prayer before the representation/skit of Christ's birth—all of which are helpfully provided in the catechesis manual.

While catechesis for the children during the visit is the focus, the volunteers also report that they receive formation in the process. "One of the strongest themes of our movement is to live the reconciliation brought by Christ," Cañola said. "Jesus became man to reconcile all men to God. I can't really be an instrument if I don't live what I preach. We have to transmit the message of reconciliation and be men and women who are coherent in our faith. We hope that those who join up with us in *Navidad es Jesús* don't miss the opportunity to reconcile themselves with Jesus."

Johanna Gutiérrez, a young woman in Peru, said her faith was challenged and changed thanks to her participation in *Navidad es Jesús*: "About six years ago, a friend invited me to participate in *Navidad es Jesús*. I have always liked to help and I accepted immediately. We began to prepare a campaign for 3,000 children and it caught my attention that everything was very well organized, we had a manual, defined functions. I asked myself who brought this to fruition, what was *Navidad es Jesús*? My friend explained that it was part of a very large movement called MVC, which helped thousands of children during Christmas.

"She invited me to a large celebration after the campaigns were done and there I met many people who weren't afraid to express what I was also feeling, the desire to know Jesus better.

"It had been a long time since I had confessed and I was embarrassed that I didn't even know which words to use to confess but my friend helped me and gave me the strength to do it. That was my breaking point and the priest told me, 'The heavens are throwing a party because a daughter has returned.' I left with teary eyes and began to pray as when I was a child.

"The next year, my friend had to travel and she left me with the task of organizing the *Navidad es* Jesús visit. Since then, I am in charge every year of organizing a *Navidad* visit for 3,000 children, recruiting more volunteers each time, because I know there are so many people who, like me, just need a hand and someone who will help me become closer to Jesus."

## Christmas Rings Through the Year

As Cañola explains, all those who participate are called to "service and sanctity." As such, volunteers often organize Advent reflections leading up to their scheduled *Navidad es Jesús* visit to combat the busyness and hyperactivity of the Advent and Christmas seasons. Volunteer meetings prior to the visit are a mix of spiritual retreat and logistical preparation. The message that is stressed is that "we do what we do because we are Christian, we are Catholic, and we want to transmit the true reason for Christmas," Cañola said.

Immediately after the visits, volunteers are invited to continue participating in MVC events, such as Christmas Eve Mass, Christmas caroling, praying the Advent wreath together, and more. They are also encouraged to send thank-you cards to the sponsors of their visits and their main collaborators, and are invited to a large celebratory party with all the volunteers in the program.

Because of the sense of community they feel, many volunteers begin to make friends with MVC members. Eventually many join the movement and participate in the community's activities all through the year. Some are also encouraged to assume leadership roles at the following year's *Navidad es Jesús* visits and many do so, because they feel supported and encouraged by the MVC community and don't feel out of their depth in a leadership position, thanks to the detailed manuals.

"We are committed, faithful lay people that they happened to encounter through *Navidad es Jesús*," said Cañola. "In MVC, they find a movement that has life. Many continue serving in the same areas they visited at Christmas and develop a relationship with the neighborhood. People find that living their faith is more than just attending Mass. They find a community of people who live out their faith beyond that."

## Infusing the Mainstream with Grace

The *Navidad es Jesús* campaign has found innovative and effective ways of penetrating the secular culture. Because their volunteers live the faith that they preach at *Navidad es Jesús* visits, they are passionate about the message, making them very effective at promotions.

"We find ourselves in a cultural battle," said Cañola. "Peru is a Catholic country with very Catholic roots, but we are confronted with very secular ideas. Slowly, though, the idea of *Navidad es Jesús* is taking hold. Instead of pictures of Santa Claus on businesses, we are now finding the Holy Family. Things are changing."

For starters, governments in small towns and neighborhoods are adopting the phrase, *"Navidad es Jesús"* in their Christmas greetings and government holiday signs. Radio Programas del Peru (or Radio RPP for short), the largest radio station in Peru, is using *Navidad es Jesús* as its theme. The main newspaper in the country also promotes the *Navidad es Jesús* campaign. And Coca Cola in Peru once sponsored a *Navidad es Jesús* Christmas CD that had widespread distribution throughout the country.

*Navidad es Jesús* posters are prominently displayed throughout Lima. Many have prayers on them and have contact information for people to receive more information about Christmas. The message on the posters appeals to many readers because it calls upon people to serve others in the face of "the suffering of our brothers in need," said Cañola. *Navidad es Jesús* once sponsored a large nativity scene in the center of Lima, and the chief organizer in charge of making it happen, who happened to be Jewish, was instrumental to its success.

"Living nativities" (using actors) are also being conducted by *Navidad es Jesús* teams in Ecuador. "In 2011, we did living nativities in the streets of the cities of Guayaquil and Manta and were very well received by drivers and passersby as they recalled that the real meaning of Christmas is the birth of Christ Jesus, who became a child out of love for us," said Erika Chacón Maldonado, director of public relations for *Fundación Acción Solidaria* (Solidarity Action Foundation), which is run by MVC members in Ecuador and is the equivalent to Peru's *Solidaridad en Marcha*.

Many *Navidad es Jesús* volunteers are also very active in promoting the cause in the months leading up to Christmas. They run a variety of fundraising campaigns, such as selling *Navidad es Jesús* polo shirts, bracelets, ornaments, and nativity sets. "These things begin generating interest in the program," said Cañola.

Widespread interest in restoring the religious meaning of overly commercialized holidays has been spreading thanks to the efforts of MVC movement. Because of *Navidad es Jesús*" success during Christmas, some volunteers this year started *Semana Santa es Jesus* (Holy Week is Jesus) campaigns, and others launched spiritual campaigns during Valentine's Day as well.

A group of employees at a Walmart-type store in Peru who volunteer yearly for *Navidad es Jesús* approached the organizers and asked them to come in to give a series of reflections during Holy Week. "It's interesting because the message is spreading beyond the parishes and allowing Christ to even enter workplaces," said Cañola.

As more and more people get involved in the movement, Cañola explained, their friends and acquaintances come to think of them as a representative of their faith and come to talk to them to get their perspective. Canola offers an example: "One employee at a coffee shop I frequent, who I met through *Navidad es Jesús*, expressed to me one day that she had been cohabiting with the same man for many years and they had three children together but she wanted to get married in the Church. She approached me and asked me how to go about doing this since she knows me to be a person of faith."

Another related campaign sponsored by *Navidad es Jesús* to generate greater interest in the group's work is the annual National Nativity Contest. *Navidad es Jesús* has teamed up with *El Instituto Cultural Teatral y Social* (the Cultural, Theater and Social Institute) in Peru to invite artists to create handmade nativity scenes. Retreats and art workshops are offered for the artists, so that well-crafted art reflects its religious roots. Many businesses then purchase the nativities and display them at their offices; others are sold in shopping malls. This is a success in itself, says Cañola, because good religious art isn't being relegated to small street markets, but is being sold side-by-side with more commercialized Christmas items in the major shopping malls.

Other *Navidad es Jesús* cultural ventures have included contests for music, poetry and Christmas stories. Brazil's *Navidad es Jesús* program (which is currently found only in the city of Petrópolis) features an annual nationwide Christmas-story contest called "*Histórias de Natal*." MVC organizes the contest, founded in 2003, as an effort to evangelize the culture. "We receive an average of 250 stories each year," explained Martín Ugarteche Fernández, who is in charge of the annual contest. "There is a team of twenty people who put this on and help judge the entries, including members of *Movimiento de Vida Cristiana*, professors and alumni of the Catholic University of Petrópolis, and academics from the Petrópolis Academy of Letters."

A compilation book including the stories written by previous years' finalists is now in print, and a second volume will be published in 2013. *Histórias de Natal* has received official support from the World Youth Day Rio 2013 organizing committee, and the 2012 writing theme coincides with the theme of World Youth Day: "Go and make disciples of all nations" (Matt 28:19) to help young people prepare both for Christmas and the papal visit. Contest submissions have already been received from all over Brazil and the total number of submissions is expected to reach 500 this year. "*Histórias de Natal* complements the work of *Navidad es Jesús*," said Ugarteche Fernández. "Both have as their objectives to evangelize Christmas, announcing a profound spiritual meaning and encouraging people to live in greater solidarity."

## Successes and Challenges

Although it is difficult to estimate how many people—both those who are being served and those who have served—have benefited from their participation in *Navidad es Jesús*, Cañola counts among the greatest successes of the project the fact that it is "a gateway to persevere in faith." He explains: "We are grateful for the possibility to enter in the midst of society, raise people up, and bring them to the faith. It permits us to extend a hand from the Church and reach people in businesses and at universities and allow them to have a faith experience that benefits others. There is much joy in this and it is contagious; it is an invitation to live a Christian life."

For *Navidad es Jesús* in Costa Rica, the successes have been many. The program has formally existed there since 2005, although prior to that MVC members were hosting Christmas parties to begin spreading awareness about the true meaning of the season. Today the visits model those in Peru and members generally visit between 5,000 and 8,000 children throughout Costa Rica each year. The community there is also proud that university students organized a *Navidad es Jesús* visit in 2010 in the neighboring country of Nicaragua, in the capital city of Managua.

"In general, the campaign has been for us an opportunity to take Christ Jesus to everyone, an occasion to share the joy and even the struggles in the Christian life," said Fabiola Ramirez, who has been involved in *Navidad es Jesús* in Costa Rica since its inception. He adds, "Through this campaign that we have carried on throughout these twelve years, we have brought joy to more than 80,000 children, we have visited the country's twelve provinces, from border to border, and we have also been able to meet with our Nicaraguan brothers. Above all, the fruits have been the immense joy in our hearts, not of giving something, but instead Someone: He who is the reason for our true joy."

Challenges still exist, however. Ramirez admits: "For us, the greatest challenge is at the level of catechesis and evangelization, since society heavily promotes consumerism and materialism, and breaking through this message in the minds of children is complicated. Additionally, it is always a challenge to financially cover the costs of campaign logistics."

In Peru, Cañola shares Ramirez's frustration about the cultural battle with consumerism and the inability to reach everyone with the real Christmas message. He also wishes there were more tools, more means, and more ways to reach more people. But even amid some challenges, he said, God always acts. He explained that some *Navidad es Jesús* visits are better organized than others, and generally speaking, adults have activities planned out in advance whereas younger members sometimes procrastinate when preparing their Christmas visits. At one visit, university students were coordinating a visit for 700 children at a site about two hours away. Although the volunteers did not realize it, only half of the children's gifts were packed up into the bus; the other half remained behind underneath a table at the university. Fortunately a group of adults were doing a *Navidad es Jesús* campaign nearby and when they were contacted to see if they happened to have extra gifts, they had more than enough—they had brought more, just in case, and all the children at both sites received gifts.

Cañola also would like to see the campaign taken to Europe. There are MVC members there—primarily in Italy and England—but no *Navidad es Jesús* campaigns. He thinks these countries could greatly benefit from these campaigns, especially since many people there are in spiritual need and have lost sight of the true meaning of Christmas.

During this Year of Faith, *Navidad es Jesús* organizers want to focus more on the cultural dynamic. They are already in negotiations with Peru's largest newspaper, radio stations, and other media to have ongoing messages run throughout Peru—especially in places where the group isn't present—about the project. They want to make sure people don't forget why this campaign is underway.

"We also want members of this community to be leaven, to be spokespeople for *Navidad es Jesús* year round," Cañola said. "Most of our members are busy with work or studies and need to be reminded that it's not just the children who need the message of Christmas. They, too, need to intensely live Jesus so that others around them may do so as well."

*Angelique Ruhi-López, MA, is the co-author of* The Infertility Companion for Catholics: Spiritual and Practical Support for Couples *and is a freelance writer and web editor for the Archdiocese of Miami. She is a wife and the mother of five children. To learn more about Christmas is Jesus, see www.navidadesjesus.org.*

CHAPTER FIVE

# Kenyan Street Kids Learn of Cows and Catechisms

*Moses Muthaka with Conor Donnolly*

My aunt's cow was due to give birth. My aunt is a widow, elderly and diabetic. The eight young men who live on a neighboring farm offered to help. They told her to go to bed; they would the look after the delivery. She was overjoyed at the offer and at how these fellows could handle the situation now, as she is feeling the weight of her years. Her only cow is quite a treasure and an important source of income. Her own children have long since emigrated to the city, and she has no one to help with the usual farm chores. So the involvement of these neighbors, to the point that they were able to handle the calf's delivery, was a real godsend.

The farm land is a lush fertile, green area about two hours outside Nairobi. It is one of the best farming areas in the country and quite beautiful. The area is populated by many small *shambas* or farms, which mostly grow tea, and keep one cow and a few chickens. As there is not much land for grazing; the system used is called "zero grazing." This means that the grass is cut by humans and brought on a daily basis to the cow, which is kept in a small space. It is an economical system; this way small farmers do not need much land in order to rear cows.

These boys from the farm near my aunt's are no ordinary kids. They come from a slum area of Nairobi. I met them when we first went to explore the plot of land, which we were buying for a technical school in Eastlands. They were street kids. Some lived in shanties with their parents, five to a room, with a clay floor and a corrugated iron roof. Others were orphans and slept wherever they could—some on the side of the road, some in a hole in the ground with a plastic cover for a roof when it rained, which was often. They survived by collecting scrap metal, newspaper, and plastic and managed to eke out a living selling the scraps. Usually they would have only one meal a day and so they were always hungry.

Today, a group of these young people work hard and live with dignity on the land, thanks to the efforts of a Catholic apostolate that was founded to give slum-dwellers the skills they need for success and independence. But the road these young people took was an unexpected one, which offers lessons for anyone interested in helping the poor become self-sufficient—lessons about the centrality of family, and of re-establishing bonds between young and old, the city and the countryside.

## From Yale to Colonial Kenya

The story of my aunt and the cows and the helpful neighbors began in the 1950s in Connecticut, where a Protestant Yale undergraduate by the name of David Sperling became intrigued by what he read about the Catholic faith, and eventually came to accept it. He met some members of an organization that was almost new to the United States, Opus Dei, and found in it his vocation—to serve as a "numerary" (lay celibate) member. By the late 1950s he was studying in Rome, with regular exposure to the group's founder, Msgr. Josemaría Escrivá, who would later be canonised by Pope John Paul II.

It was Escrivá himself who asked Sperling to go to Kenya to advance the work of Opus Dei, which had put down roots there in 1958. By 1961, Sperling and a few other team members had started a school for boys—the first interracial school in segregated British East Africa. The school was named Strathmore, after the road where it was located. Today Strathmore University, a corporate work of Opus Dei, is one of the finest universities in East Africa.

Strathmore has long been concerned with promoting economic development, and in January 2003 it started a new initiative aimed at the people of a very low-income Nairobi neighborhood, Eastlands. Formerly a segregated section where African employees of white-owned businesses lived, Eastlands makes up a sizable part of the city, and it is mostly made up of one-room dwellings. Many Eastlands residents work in the informal business sector, or *juakali* (in Swahili, literally "under the sun"), in low-paid, low-skill "day jobs." To offer these workers training in higher-level skills, and help match them with employers, Strathmore launched the Informal Sector Business Institute. I began work there as marketing manager, in charge of helping the Institute connect with potential trainees.

Through these practical, hands-on courses, priests and other members of Opus Dei came into contact with young potential entrepreneurs. In the first decade of operation the Institute has trained 6,000 people in business skills—but even more importantly, has attracted many of the students to programs of spiritual formation: regular meditations, days of recollection, and retreats. Parenting talks for married couples and family-enrichment courses were started on Saturday afternoons. A monthly day of recollection, conducted in Swahili, became part of the program.

## The Children of the Street

As part of the Institute's outreach, we were building a new school in Eastlands—and that is where I came to know so many street kids. We had discovered some twenty-five of them who "lived rough" near the new school's site—making their living by searching in garbage for plastic and metal they could collect and sell. All were orphans, abandoned by their parents, ranging in age from nine to twenty-two. They slept on cardboard boxes and used sacks as blankets. We asked them what we could do for them: All they requested from us were large plastic sheets to keep out the rain.

We realized that these very kids were the population we hoped to help through the school we were building. Some had been to primary school, others had missed many years for lack of tuition. Some were Catholic but with little formation; others had not been baptized.

Some friends from Singapore who were visiting Nairobi agreed to host a lunch for some of the street kids, who were skeptical at first. One who sat at my table, told me: "Today we are very lucky. Usually we eat from the dustbin." Another said, "No one has ever given us anything before." What was most striking about these uneducated youths was their exquisite courtesy and good manners. All were effusive in their thanks, expressed in the local Swahili, *asante sana*.

In time, we managed to set up a shelter for the children, so that at least they had a real roof over their heads. We called it Shalom. We next tried to get some back into school. There were ups and downs, successes and failures. It became apparent that if we were to make real progress we needed to get them out of the environment of the slum—where poverty and hopelessness grind people down so hard that some of them despair, and view their own children as crushing burdens that they must abandon.

I come from a family of eleven. All of us have grown up and moved away from the farm where we were born. My father passed away a few years ago and so my mother is alone. I convinced Mum to try, as an experiment, giving shelter to a selected group of these kids. My mother can neither read nor write, but having reared a large family in tough circumstances, she is made of steel and has a youthful spirit of adventure, so she was willing to give it a try. We started with some apprehensions. There were many adjustments to be made, not least of which was the fact that these kids speak a different dialect and so initially they had to communicate with Mum by sign language. I work in Nairobi, quite some distance away, so I could only be in contact by phone.

We managed to get some school fees from foreign donations. We received clothes for the fellows from local supporters. (These boys needed absolutely everything. Where I come from even a pencil is a treasure, not to mention a copy book.) So they began to attend the local school. Being an experienced farm manager and self-taught psychologist, my mother made sure the boys had no spare time. After school they had to collect the grass for the cow, milk the cow, feed the chickens, sweep the yard, pick the tea, and a number of other tasks. We were anxious at first to see how chores would work out for these city kids with their new and demanding taskmistress. Some could not keep up the pace, and returned to Nairobi to their old life, but the majority have stuck it out.

The first thing the boys noticed was the value of three solid, guaranteed meals a day. They were also overjoyed at the prospect of going to school—an opportunity that so many of their old friends would never have.

We then began to notice that my mother would occasionally come for visits to Nairobi and leave the boys in charge of the farm. She felt she could trust them. There was slight hiccup when after one of these trips she discovered feathers of one of her chickens. The official story was that it was hit by a football during an ongoing soccer match and so it *just* had to be eaten!

Among the group, leaders began to emerge which ones could be counted on to control, lead, and inspire the others. James, Anthony and Ezechiel were the first to shine. They were followed by Boniface, Duncan, Joseph and Dennis.

My neighbouring uncles and aunts were so impressed by the new recruits that they asked if they could invite some young men to stay at their houses too. (In most cases their own children had grown up and moved to Nairobi, leaving them all alone.) There are now some sixteen boys in local boarding schools who descend on my Mum's farm for the holidays. Their new rural home is much more wholesome than the slums of Nairobi, and so is the prospect of three meals a day!

## Spiritual Formation and My Mum

My mother shepherds these boys to Mass every Sunday. Those who had previously had no religion, when asked if they wanted to go to church, replied that they wanted to go to the "Church of Moses" (i.e., the one I went to). Many are now receiving catechism classes in preparation for baptism. When passing by their rooms recently, I was surprised to overhear them reciting the rosary. Last August they painted the fence of the local church, again under the direction of my Mum.

Those who were baptized Catholics have all now been confirmed. They go to Sunday Mass in the small local chapel and sing. (They learned Christmas carols last Advent.) All have gone through a three-day silent retreat. We are in the process of trying to organize regular opportunities for confession. When the priest from Nairobi comes to visit, three hours away, they are eager to have a session of spiritual direction. Some have read the writings of the saints—simple things, but they surprise us sometimes with the passages they can quote. The rosary is part of their daily schedule.

We offer talks on the virtues for the boys once a month and they listen attentively. Lately they have begun to bring their friends from school and the neighboring area. We are encouraging them to reach out to their friends in class. The Year of Faith (2012-2013) offers endless possibilities for them to evangelize more people in the area. Two seminarians from Madrid visited them recently, and they are planning a work camp for seminarians next year, in which the seminarians can spend time teaching more catechism classes to all these fellows and the children in the region.

What is also surprising about this group is that the boys are from different tribes. Tribal differences are a major source of conflict in Kenya—for instance, the post-election violence in 2007. However it is not a problem with these fellows, partly thanks to their Christian formation.

They are eager to learn. All have done well at school. Two are at the top of their class; four or five look as if they can make it to university; two are class captains or class prefects; one is the captain of the soccer team. My mum—whom they call *shu shu*, Kikuyu for "grandmother"—makes sure they can look after themselves. So they all now know how to cook, particularly their favourites, *ugali* and *chapati*, common local dishes made from maize flour.

For my birthday last week they did all the cooking, supervised by Mum, for my three friends who accompanied me "upcountry" to see them. In the get-together they were all very talkative, joking with each other—clearly feeling at home. (Last year on a similar occasion they hardly spoke.) It is impressive to see all the agricultural and domestic skills they have acquired in just a year or two and how my Mum has trained them. She keeps them busy during the holidays but leaves them some time for soccer. They can watch the small TV, but only during the holidays.

We have encouraged the boys to see how they can help the other local farmers—most of them elderly. Dealing with cows in labor, and otherwise assisting elderly farmers, is not traditionally listed among the corporal works of mercy; but if St. Matthew had lived in Muranga it might have been!

We are planning for the future. One fellow asked recently if when the boys finish school, they could stay together, since they feel like they are a family. That inspired the idea of a family farm school in Muranga, where the boys could be resident managers. It's unclear if that will work out. But the experience of transferring abandoned street kids from a toxic slum to a wholesome rural area, and connecting them with lonely members of the older generation, has shown everyone involved just how many possibilities there are for doing good and spreading the Gospel in unexpected ways. The world is full of need, and full of ways of meeting it. You just need eyes to see, and ears to listen.

*Moses Muthaka is marketing manager at the Informal Sector Business Institute in Nairobi, Kenya. Conor Donnelly is a priest of the Prelature of Opus Dei, also in Nairobi.*

CHAPTER SIX

# Music Fuels a Catholic Rebirth in Vladivostok

*Philip F. Lawler*

WHEN HE WAS A YOUNG MAN, Rev. Daniel Mauer recalls, neighbors accused him of breaking into a local church simply so that he could play the organ. I notice, during our telephone conversation, that he simply reports those accusations; he does not deny them. But if he was guilty, it was a victimless crime, and the statute of limitations protects him. True or false, the charges establish his longstanding interest in church organs. So it is ironic, although probably not coincidental, that today Rev. Mauer serves as a missionary in Vladivostok, in a parish that is drawing attention throughout the Russian Far East because of its organ concerts.

Before the Revolution, the parish of Most Holy Mother of God in Vladivostok boasted 15,000 Catholic parishioners: mostly native Poles who had found work in the Pacific port city. But like most churches it was desecrated by the Bolsheviks, then confiscated. The Militant Atheists' League rampaged through the building, destroying thousands of icons. In their ideological frenzy, the young vandals were chipping away at a large white-marble crucifix that had stood behind the altar, knocking the fingers off the figure of Christ, when a quick-thinking witness suggested that the sculpture could serve as an anatomy model for art students. The crucifix was spared, donated to a local art academy, and in 1996 it was finally returned to the parish.

For years the empty church served Communist government officials as a repository for official archives. After the fall of the Communist regime, the Russian Federation enacted laws ordering the return of churches to their original congregations. But in Vladivostok, government officials had already made new plans for the church building; it was to be converted into an orchestra hall. The process would involve relocating the archives to a new site and removing the interior floors that had been added to the building. Work began in the 1980s, then slowed to a halt as the Soviet economy collapsed and funding for the renovation dried up.

In 1992, two missionaries from the United States arrived in Vladivostok. Rev. Myron Effing and then-Brother

Daniel Mauer, members of the Canons Regular of Jesus the Lord, had received legal permission for their work because a Catholic parish had already been established in the city before the Revolution. A local political official, recalling his parents' involvement, had taken out advertisements to locate former parishioners, and produced a list of fifteen surviving members of the Catholic community.

As he negotiated with government officials for the return of the parish church, Rev. Effing encountered the objection that the building was no longer available, since it had been designated as a future site for musical concerts. He countered by saying that if the building were returned to the Catholic Church, an organ would be installed and concerts would be open to the public. That argument helped overcome opposition, and on January 1, 1994, Rev. Effing formally received the keys to the building. Most Holy Mother of God parish was the first Catholic church in Russia to be restored to Catholic ownership.

However, one significant obstacle stood in the path of the plan to host organ concerts in the parish. The church didn't have an organ.

### The First Transplanted Organ

Later in 1994, during a fundraising trip back to the United States, Rev. Mauer was visiting the Church of the Epiphany of the Lord in Coon Rapids (a suburb of Minneapolis) Minnesota, when he noticed an abandoned electric organ. The Minnesota parish had upgraded, purchasing a superior instrument, and had found no interested buyers for the classic Rodgers Cambridge 220-II. When Rev. Mauer expressed interest, the parish volunteered to donate the instrument to the mission in Vladivostok—and pay for its transportation as well. Employing the wisdom of serpents, Rev. Effing persuaded local officials that no tax duties should be imposed on the import, since the organ was required for the government-approved mission of the parish to hold public concerts.

Arriving in Vladivostok in mid-1995, the organ was kept in a warehouse while renovations continued at the church. By the end of the year the interior floors and walls had been removed, the original worship space had been restored, and a choir loft had been prepared for the organ's installation.

Just one more obstacle remained: there was no organist. The instrument installed at Most Holy Mother of God parish was the first classical organ to be seen in the Russian Far East (a region roughly 1.5 times the size of the continental United States). There were no organists in the parish, and no qualified organ instructors to be found within 4,000 miles.

Marina Omelchenko was hired in 1995 as the parish "organist"—in reality, the music director. At the time she had never even seen an organ. A skilled musician, she is the child of a noted concert flutist and an operatic soprano. Trained as a pianist, she had recently graduated from the Russian Far Eastern Institute of Arts in Vladivostok.

During her first months at the parish she played for liturgical services on a small tabletop keyboard.

Once the organ was installed in the church, Marina began teaching herself to play it, with the help of English-language textbooks. Starting with the most basic setps, she learned how to turn on the instrument and how to change the registration (organ stops). Soon she was the first musician in Vladivostok to play the organ on a regular basis. During the summer of 1996 an American organist, Susan Gray, visited Vladivostok and gave Marina her first actual lessons, teaching her about the organ's registration and the special legato touch that the instrument requires. By November Marina was ready to offer her first public concert.

The first organ concert—not just for Most Holy Mother of God parish, but for Vladivostok and for the Russian Far East—was held on November 24, 1996, to celebrate the return of the parish's historic marble crucifix. Organized by a parishioner, Ludmila Rakhmanova, the concert also included performances by the Cantabile Chamber Choir of the Far Eastern Symphony Orchestra, by the Ensemble of Ancient Music, and by a flutist and a soprano. But the organ music was particularly well received. Rev. Effing and Rev. Mauer quickly recognized an opportunity for evangelization. Russians love music, but the treasures of sacred music had been forbidden to them during more than sixty years of officially atheistic rule. By treating them to such beautiful, alien music, the priests realized, they could introduce people to the Christian faith.

## Functional Atheism

In theory Russians should already be well acquainted with Christianity. The Russian Orthodox Church, which dominates the nation's religious life, insists that Russia is Christian country. But decades of official atheism—and of Orthodox cooperation with the regime—have taken their toll. Today few Russians are educated in the faith and fewer still are regular in attending religious services.

During the Soviet era the number of Russians baptized as Christians fell to less than 10 percent of the population. Since the fall of the Communist regime it has rebounded, and the Moscow Patriarchate claims the allegiance of a majority of Russian citizens. But actual church attendance figures belie that claim. In the region around Vladivostok, about three-quarters of the population is now baptized. But only about 1 percent attend church services on a regular basis.

Along with the decline in religious practice, Russia has seen a catastrophic breakdown in family life. Drunkenness is epidemic, abortion rates are astronomical, and a staggering 94 percent of all marriages end in divorce—in 80 percent of those cases, within just four years after the marriage!

In practice, then, Russia is mission territory. Yet the Vatican carefully avoids using that term, fearful of offending the Russian Orthodox Church, which (again, on paper) is by far the largest of the world's Orthodox bodies, and thus the Vatican's premier partner in ecumenical dialogue. The Moscow Patriarchate jealously guards all of Russia as its "canonical territory," and is quick to complain if Catholic clerics appear to be "stealing sheep" from Orthodox flocks—even if those flocks are inactive.

While *perestroika* brought new life to the Orthodox Church, the 1980s saw a rise in tensions between Moscow and Rome, which continued after the collapse of Communism. Blessed John Paul II was viewed with deep suspicions by many Russians, who could only see the late Pontiff's desire to visit Moscow as a new outcropping of historic Polish ambitions on Russian territory. The Orthodox hierarchy, with its persistent complaints about Catholic "proselytism" in historically Orthodox communities, tacitly encouraged that hostility.

Meanwhile the sudden demand for Orthodox priests, to staff the parishes that were reopened under *perestroika*, produced a new generation of clerics who had been trained hastily, and had absorbed little more than the Old Slavonic language of the liturgy and the traditional Orthodox hostility toward Catholicism. In many cases the young priests proved to be opportunists, anxious to secure an easy living and resentful of anything that they saw as competition. To complicate matters, these young priests also had a tendency to alienate their parishioners. The historic complicity of the Orthodox Church with the Communist regime, now followed by the transparent corruption of many Orthodox priests, nourished a deep popular cynicism about the Moscow Patriarchate in particular, and religion in general.

## Leaving Coats on the Altar

When Most Holy Mother of God church began hosting musical performances, many of those in attendance reported that it was their first-ever visit to a Christian church. In fact their behavior testified to their ignorance of elementary church etiquette. Some concert-goers brought food and drink into the church; some left their coats on the altar. Still, the response was enthusiastic, and the missionary priests persevered—doing their best to provide some guidance in proper decorum for future concerts.

The first concert in November 1996 drew a crowd of 500, roughly twice the capacity of the church. When two subsequent concerts produced roughly equal crowds, the parish saw the need to require tickets—not to raise revenues (the concerts remained free of charge) but simply to limit attendance. Soon it became necessary to schedule multiple performance of each concert. Within two years, the parish concert program became the most successful series of musical performances in the history of Vladivostok.

Gradually, some of the concert-goers began to recognize the link between the beauty of the sacred music and the truths of the faith. Some began inquiring about Catholicism; ten people began to undertake instruction in the faith. (Among the first converts attracted by the music program was Marina Omelchenko, the parish organist, who was baptized at the Easter Vigil in 1996.) Father Mauer hesitates to give the concerts full credit for these conversions; he suggests that the newly baptized Catholics "had it in the back of their minds" to explore the faith, even before they heard the organ music. Still he has no doubt that the concerts have succeeded in "raising the religious consciousness of the people" who attend.

From 2000 to the present—with a long break for final church renovations in 2006-2007—the parish has presented twelve to eighteen public organ concerts and recitals each year, and many more concerts organized for private groups. In addition to the traditional Christmas and Easter concerts, the parish has organized and performed concerts in honor of the parish patroness the Most Holy Mother of God on the feast of her birth (September 8); several special "Ave Maria" concerts during the Marian month of May; *Requiem* concerts and *Stabat Mater* concerts during Lent to remember solemnly the suffering of Jesus and his mother; and concerts to present various kinds of organ music or to mark special events in the history of the parish, such as the re-consecration of the church in February 2008.

In December 2003 the Vladivostok mission received another generous gift from an American parish. Stella

Maris church in Sullivan's Island, South Carolina donated a large Trillium 927 organ that used the latest digital electronic technology to imitate the sounds of real pipes. With ninety-four speaking stops, the new instrument was one of the largest concert organs in Russia. In 2008 the parish added a set of set of Fratelli Ruffatti winded pipes. With this large and complex new organ of total of 177 stops the parish organ concert series took a big step forward. Instead of depending solely on parish organists to learn many new programs of organ music each year, the parish now invited the best organists from throughout Russia and from around the world to give recitals and concerts.

The enormous popularity of the concert series was a sign that Marina Omelchenko would need more formal instruction as an organist. In 2003 she received a grant to study in the United States, under David Jenkins, the director of liturgical music at St. Paul seminary in Minnesota. The following year she became working as a "distance learning" student with Alexei Parshin of the Tchaikovsky Conservatory in Moscow. In 2006 she enrolled in a professional music program at the University of Graz, Austria, but continued to return to Vladivostok regularly for parish concerts. Since 2006 she has also been head organist at the Roman Catholic cathedral of the Immaculate Conception in Moscow, and since 2010 she has been organ soloist for the Beijing International Chamber Orchestra. She has added an international concert schedule, including appearances in Austria, Hungary,

Germany, Poland, Italy, France, Spain, the Czech Republic, and China, as well as many cities in Russia. In the summer of 2012 she made her first concert tour of the United States, playing a solo concert program appropriately entitled "'Awake, My Soul!'– Russia Responds to Sacred Organ Music."

From a musical perspective the success of the parish organ concerts is unquestionable. But from the perspective of evangelization as well, the parish of Most Holy Mother of God counts the concerts as a major success. For sixteen years, concert-goers have reported that their faith in Jesus Christ has been strengthened and deepened—or perhaps awakened for the first time—by the beautiful sounds of the sacred music, and the reverent surroundings of the church in which the music is played.

Only a small minority of those who have appreciated the organ concerts have chosen to explore the Catholic faith. But a foundation has been established for those who might later wish to learn more about Catholicism. For others, Father Mauer observes, the concerts are "helping them to understand their Orthodox faith." All in all, the concerts have provided the most successful means by which American missionaries in the Russian Far East have been able to introduce the Gospel message to a post-Christian culture.

CHAPTER SEVEN

# In Downtown Chicago, a Liturgy Glimpses Eternity

*Matthew Rarey*

WHEN I FIRST VISITED St. John Cantius Church in August 2000, the contrast between the way of beauty and the way of the modern world could not have been more jarring.

Overhead, multi-million dollar engines of warfare shrieked—the Chicago Air Show was in full force—while inside the church was filled with a symphony of choir music and the equally beautiful symphony of silence from the prayerful congregation. A visiting priest gave the homily, and he talked about the "cacophony of noise" flooding the world and distracting people from God. As if to underscore his point, he occasionally had to pause as a jet boomed above.

I made that first visit having newly graduated from Wabash College, where professor of classics David Kubiak—who introduced me and other Catholic students to the Latin Mass in Indianapolis, even instructing us in how to serve it—told me to visit my hometown treasure of the old-time Catholic faith. It would be a baptism in beauty.

I attended Mass that day with my father, and the experience made him say he would never go to another church again. (The convenience of the local parish made him renege on that promise. St. John Cantius is located just west of downtown, a deep drive into the city from the family home in the northwest suburbs.) The beauty and reverence were overwhelming for some people accustomed to the new form of the Mass, to folksy hymns, and a casual and talkative atmosphere at the sacrament which is the source and summit of the faith.

The St. John Cantius experience was not limited to the Mass, nor to the opportunity for confession at some six confessionals, each with a long lines of penitents. There is also the beauty of the church itself, as well as the collection of Church treasures on display—paintings, statuary, relics, old liturgical vessels, often rescued from other churches that no longer want them, or donated by the concerned parishioners of churches around the country that are closing.

That first visit was a feast for my soul, nourished by many return visits over the years. It also was a feast of other sorts, proving that St. John Cantius is not only a "destination church" that some people drive over two hours to attend, but a vibrant parish.

Outside the church the annual parish picnic was going on, a jar for donations being the only admittance fee. An oompah band played next to a keg of German beer, tables were laden with food, and little children—lots of them, a very healthy sign—darting around as the parish's community of priests and seminarians, the Canons Regular of St. John Cantius, stolled about in their soutanes, chatting and laughing. They also ate heartily, with the appetites of men in love with life. Sometimes they have a propensity to enjoy life a little too much, as the pastor, Rev. C. Frank Phillips, CR, and Rev. Scott A. Haynes, SJC, will readily admit. I remember Father Phillips issuing a weight-loss challenge to parishioners from the pulpit, asking them to join him in shedding some pounds.

But back to the laughter. The laughter that filled the picnic area was issuing from hearty souls in a parish that nurtures friendships, uniting people around their common love for beauty that serves the faith.

God is truth, and beauty is true. Ugliness is the mark of the beast, although the Devil has his sly ways. (Shocking people into the reality of evil would be a loser's tactic, but the biggest loser in history is wickedly intelligent.) So the Devil deploys his ugliness in a low-key, aw-shucks manner, infusing all the banality that surrounds us every day. This induces the gray spiritual indifference that makes people look downward, to focus on the here and now, rather than on ternity or its lovely echoes on earth.

Such echoes hang in the air at St. John Cantius, which follows the "way of beauty" through liturgy, music, art, and architecture, and even its own press—the wryly titled Biretta Books, which boasts a global readership. The fruits of this walk with beauty have been consistent, as the faith of the parish has deepened and drawn in worshippers from every sort of background. On Sundays the pews are filled with Catholics devoted to the traditional Latin Mass—typically large families with women wearing head coverings, but also including hipsters and the occasional hobo. Yet the parish has also drawn many non-Catholics to the flock, including (just for instance) a Muslim structural engineer who, while working at the church, was so inspired by what he saw that he sought instruction in the faith. The parish's success is a reminder of the fact that, as recently as the 1940s and 50s, one of the factors that converts reported attracted them first to the Catholic faith was the liturgy.

## Creating a Destination Church

Founded by Polish immigrants at the end of the nineteenth-century, St. John Cantius Church had hit hard times by the 1980s. Falling into disrepair as the number of parishioners dwindled to 250 because of demographic shifts in the neighborhood, the parish needed big shoulders to hoist it back up to its former glory. These arrived in the person of Rev. C. Frank Phillips, CR, who was appointed pastor of the Resurrectionist parish in 1988.

"It would be a win-win situation to make St. John Cantius a place for the renewal of sacred traditions and the music of the liturgy," said Rev. Phillips, sitting in his rectory office on a drizzly morning in early October 2012, recalling the challenge that he had faced. A burly Chicago native with short-cropped grayish hair, wearing glasses and a soutane, he recounted how a once moribund parish had become one of Chicago's "destination churches" by embracing the power of beauty to point to the good.

An organist and conductor by training himself, Rev. Phillips made it one of his first priorities as pastor to form two choirs: the Resurrection Choir, to perform sacred works by composers such as Mozart, Schubert, and Haydn; and the St. Gregory the Great Schola, which would focus on the Church's ancient liturgical music, especially Gregorian chant.

"That's how the congregation began to grow—from people hearing about the sacred music," he said. While they may have come to listen, they were enchanted by what they saw. Altough it needed repairs, the ornate interior of St. John Cantius had escaped the "wreckovations" that had ruined so many other older churches after the Second Vatican Council—which is remarkable given that the "stripping of the altars" had been carried out with extreme enthusiasm in the Archdiocese of Chicago. The Poles who built they church might have been long dead and their descendents moved out to the suburbs, but their pious craftsmanship remained intact.

So people accustomed to ordinary churches "with very little color or religious iconography, lacking statues and devotional items," encountered at St. John Cantius "a riot of color and music," said Rev. Phillips. Almost 25 years later they continue to encounter it in even more magnificent form, thanks to decades of restoration and additions, all carried out with a keen eye to preserving the church's traditional heritage.

### A Path to Rome

Quite a few people first visit St. John Cantius without any religious purpose in mind. Craig Johnson was an Episcopalian priest who, disgusted with the theological chaos that has afflicted his communion, had quit to become a museum administrator. St. John Cantius was a stopping point in a tour organized by the Art Institute of Chicago to view outstanding examples of stained glass in the city's churches, synagogues, and public buildings.

"After almost two decades of attending one decomposing Episcopal church after another I encountered St. John Cantius Church in a piece of holy irony—a stained glass window tour," recalls Johnson. "After all, what are windows for? They allow God's brilliant light in."

He returned to the church time and again. Its visual beauty, the ethereal music, and the reverent, by-the-book celebration of the sacraments started him on the path to

Rome. The disillusioned Episcopalian had considered Catholic claims. But before coming to St. John Cantius he had never seen them expressed so integrally. "The widespread liturgical experimentation and what appeared to be doctrinal confusion in the Roman Catholic Church did not pose an obvious alternative" to Anglicanism, he recalls thinking.

For others the liturgy at St. John Cantius has caused not a change but a renewal of faith. "The moment I walked in the front door, I was awestruck," recalls Paula McGuire, who was recovering from a painful divorce when she discovered the parish in 1997. "As the Mass began and everyone knelt, I was overwhelmed with emotion... love, sorrow, joy, and many many tears. I was familiar with the Latin Mass, but had never experienced what I did that Christmas and I will never forget it.

Captivated by her experience, "I returned many times" to the parish, McGuire recalls. Looking back now on her introduction to the parish, she identifies that initial impression as "the beginning of a new journey for me"—a journey that led her to a new and deeper appreciation for her Catholic faith.

## The Mass of So Many Saints

Famous for its attention to the sacred arts, St. John Cantius is known best of all for championing the ancient liturgy of the Roman Catholic Church. Almost simultaneous with Rev. Phillips' appointment as pastor, Blessed John Paul II issued his motu proprio *Ecclesia Dei*, which granted bishops the discretion to decide when the traditional Latin Mass—now officially known as the Extraordinary Form of the Roman Rite—could be celebrated in their dioceses. When the late Cardinal Joseph Bernardin, then the Archbishop of Chicago, asked Rev. Phillips if he would mind celebrating the Latin Mass. at St. John Cantius, the priest readily agreed.

"Once we initiated the Latin Mass, the congregation really began to grow," he recounted. St. John Cantius would become a focal point of attention for Latin Mass devotees nationwide. Today the church has some 2,000 families and individuals registered as parishioners. Many of these parishioners take classes in Latin, Greek, and Hebrew.

One of those who found a home in St. John Cantius is a twenty-nine-year-old graduate student at the University of Chicago's elite Committee on Social Thought. Antón Barba-Kay, brought up in Mexico by non-Christian parents, was only baptized and confirmed in 2008. He said that attending the parish exploded his Protestant-influenced notion that "'mere' beauty is inessential to the experience at worship." As the young scholar explains:

> Cantius, of all parishes I have ever attended, exemplifies what has always impressed me most about the Catholic Church—namely, that we understand what it means to have a body. That we know there are places of earth that should be sanctified and set aside for worship, that cathedrals and churches should be erected there with

no expense spared, decorations lavished on them, the most beautiful music composed—and all so that the faithful can come together a few hours each week and look up into an image of divine majesty. It may be a pale and cheap image, but it involves all of the senses and the imagination in such a way that the mind alone is incapable of replicating, even with all the right thoughts and words. This does not change the fact that where two or more are gathered, there, too, he is. But the adornments participate and collaborate with the "thing itself" much more intimately than the analytic mind is in a position to grant. I will always be grateful to Cantius for being the trestle upon which my fledgling faith could begin to grow into this realization, the realization that the glory of God bodies forth into presence during every Mass. One must do no more at Cantius than close one's eyes to hear the hierarchies of angels singing "Sanctus! Sanctus! Sanctus!" and as the priest speaks the Latin words that burn bright with the accumulated prayers of 2,000 years, it is impossible not to feel the palpable demonstration that *'pleni sunt coeli et terra gloria tua,'* the palpable presence of the communion of saints.

In 2007 Pope Benedict XVI issued *Summorum Pontificum*, granting pastors the right to celebrate the Latin Mass without requiring the local bishop's approval. To meet the resulting surge in interest, St. John Cantius produced a set of DVDs, instructions on the parish web site (www.cantius.org), and classes at the archdiocesan seminary to provide training for priests interested in learning to celebrate Mass according to the ancient rite. Priests have another aid in the latest title from Biretta Books, *The Mystical Theology of the Mass*. Written by Rev. Haynes with an introduction by Raymond Cardinal Burke, the prefect of the Apostolic Signatura, it helps priests (and laymen) appreciate the deeper symbolism of the Extraordinary Form. To date, some 1,800 priests have learned how to offer the traditional Mass through the ministries of this parish church, which once seemed destined for the wrecking ball.

## The Parish Becomes a Movement

The parish is not a one-man show. In 1999, Rev. Phillips founded the Canons Regular of St. John Cantius, a religious community of priests, brothers, and seminarians. The Canons are dedicated to "help[ing] Catholics rediscover a profound sense of the sacred through solemn liturgies, devotions, sacred art and sacred music, as well as instruction in Church heritage, catechesis, and Catholic culture in the context of parish ministry."

Today the Canons number some twenty-three seminarians, priests, and brothers. Although their home base is St. John Cantius Church, they also administer St. Peter's Church in the tiny town of Volo, Illinois, and serve as chaplains for the Missionaries of Charity, Mother Teresa's sisters, ministering to Chicago's neediest.

One of the first men ordained to the priesthood as a Canon was Rev. Scott Haynes. Brought up as a Baptist in Mississippi, he first encountered the Church as a member of his high school orchestra, which performed for Pope John Paul II at the Superdome in New Orleans during the Pontiff's visit there in 1987. Becoming a professional musician and musicologist, he took on positions as music director at several Catholic parishes, and eventually was moved to join the Church. A gentle giant of a man and prolific composer of sacred music, Father Haynes is now the music director at St. John Cantius. He relishes the opportunity to "bring people closer to God through the window of beauty," and never misses a beat when it comes to evangelizing musicians and singers through the Church's depository of sacred music. Visiting choirs from secular schools—from the University of Chicago and Indiana University to Chicago public schools—provide a captive audience.

"For many of them, this is their first time attending Mass, maybe even setting foot in a Catholic church," Rev. Haynes said, speaking in the pastor's office after

Rev. Phillips had left to attend to his other daily duties. "When they come I usually have a bit of time to welcome them to the church, show them the sacred art, explain the theology of the building and the theological implications of the architecture and how it relates to the Jewish Temple. I also give them a translation of all the things they are singing in addition to describing the history of the prayers at Mass."

It is hard to know how many of those visiting singers and musicians might have been moved to consider Catholicism, Rev. Haynes noted. It is easier to keep tabs when it comes to the parish's own choirs. Many of the singers are volunteers, and their numbers have included not only non-Catholics but Jews and agnostics. Singing the sacred music and immersing themselves in the liturgy has a contagiously Catholic effect.

Rev. Haynes gave the example of one current chorister, a young professional singer in Chicago who first came to St. John Cantius to deliver a solo performance. Like Craig Johnson, she was an Episcopalian whose first visit occasioned many returns. Asking many questions about the Catholic faith, she eventually enrolled in RCIA classes at St. John Cantius and now sings in the choir as a professional singer and professing Catholic. She is working to bring members of her family to the faith as well.

Another chorister, Nathalie Corbett, who was baptized in the parish, admits that over the years she "really didn't enjoy going to Mass every Sunday." But her attitude changed, she says, when she joined the youth choir. "I started biking there every day to join the Canons Regular at vespers and the rosary. It became a habit."

## Beauty Will Save the World

Music is a major ministry at St. John Cantius Church, involving people of all ages. The Holy Innocents Choir is composed of small children, and as they grow older, many of the children opt to continue singing in a gradation of choirs that climaxes with such adult groups as the sixty-member Resurrection Choir and Orchestra conducted by Rev. Haynes. Combined with St. John Cantius' youth ministry program, that way of beauty discovered through music has struck chords echoing far beyond the church doors, touching souls who never set foot within them.

Overseeing youth ministry is Brother Chad McCoy, a professed brother in the community, who fell in love with St. John Cantius at first sight. Brother Chad, who is now thirty-four, had an all-too-common California adolescence marked by substance abuse and hard living. (Some of his boyhood friends are already dead.) His own family came to the rescue by sending him to Magdalen College, a small Catholic school in New Hampshire. His life was straightened out through spiritual direction and formation in the faith, and it was forever changed when Rev. Phillips visited campus his senior year.

Brother Chad always had a deep appreciation for art and reverent liturgy, which he credits as the force that was always subtly disposing him toward religious life. Listening to Rev. Phillips talk about St. John Cantius parish proved inspirational. "I knew men here were on fire for Christ and I knew I wanted to be among them," he said.

"It happened surprisingly fast," he remembered. "One day I didn't have any thoughts about religious life or St. John Cantius. The next day, after listening to and talking with Father Phillips, I felt convinced this was where God was calling me. I told him so; he knew I was well-formed in the faith, and he said he'd take me." Shortly after graduating in 2001, he came to Chicago for the first time, entered the Canons Regular, and has remained there ever since. He made perpetual vows in 2006 and could pursue the priesthood, but believes his calling is that of a brother.

"God's really blessed me in my apostolic work," he said, a hefty crucifix hanging at the hip of his soutane. Much of that has to do with youth ministry. For example, he has organized the Don Bosco Boys and Girls camps in the summers; classes on serving and singing at Mass and learning the faith; and talks by lay and religious guest speakers. Many of the young people participating in these activities also sing in one of the youth choirs.

One of the parish activities that brings youth of all ages together is its pro-life ministry. The young people lead the parish's witness at pro-life rallies, including the annual. March for Life in Washington. Pro-life events in Chicago are energized by the "flash" appearance of Cantius's youth sailing in and around their "life boat" and releasing a giant rosary made of helium-filled LIFE balloons. Sometimes parishioners go to abortion clinics to pray, reciting the rosary and the Divine Mercy chaplet and singing haunting sacred melodies learned at Mass.

In fall 2011 Brother Chad recalls, he led a group of kids to a Planned Parenthood clinic in downtown Chicago. Because a lot of them also belonged to, or had graduated from, the youth choir that he directs, they also sang simple hymns. One of them, "Coventry Carol," was about King Herod's slaughter of the Holy Innocents. "A woman inside the waiting room eventually came out the door and told the kids she'd heard them singing through the window. She was moved. She had decided not to have an abortion, so she got up and left," he recalls. As he explains the event: "The truth of beauty cuts right through faulty logic or ideology and allows Christ to move hearts."

## Of What Use Is Beauty

When we moderns think of "aesthetics," we are tempted to dismiss such matters as shallow—questions of "sizzle," not "steak." Rev. Haynes explains that there's something much deeper going on: "Since the Holy Sacrifice of the Mass invites man into the beauty of Christ, the architecture, accoutrements, texts, and ceremonies of the Mass become elevated means through which the Church reveals the saving mysteries of our Catholic faith." At St. John Cantius, Father Haynes explains, the focus on beauty in the liturgy is not an end in itself:

> The beauty of Holy Mass does not rely in essence upon the splendid beauty of iconography, ornate vestments, Gregorian chant or Baroque architecture; the Mass celebrated by a military chaplain in the trenches as whirling bombs are sounding is as much the Mass as when the Pope offers the Holy Sacrifice at the Bernini altar of Saint Peter's basilica in Rome. Yet because man's soul is lifted by beauty, the Church has invested her patrimony in fostering these sacred arts. God has placed a legitimate desire in the human soul to create beautiful things because He wants man to share in his masterpiece of creation: a creation that is good and beautiful.

*Matthew A. Rarey is a Chicago-based journalist and education consultant. St. John Cantius Church has been one of his chief joys for the past twelve years.*

**CHAPTER EIGHT**

# Persecuted Indian Christians Evangelize...by Forgiving

*Anto Akkara*

*S*O IN THE PRESENT CASE *I tell you, keep away from these men and let them alone; for if this plan or this undertaking is of men, it will fail; but if it is of God, you will not be able to overthrow them.* (Acts 5:38-39)

In late 2008, a brutal wave of anti-Christian violence engulfed the jungles of Kandhamal, in India's Orissa state. Churches were desecrated and destroyed, Christians hounded out, their houses were plundered and torched. While more than 100 Christians became martyrs for their faith, hundreds of others were brutally tortured for refusing to renounce their faith. Over 300 churches and 6,000 Christian houses were reduced to ashes or badly damaged, leaving more than 56,000 Christians homeless. Most of the survivors became refugees in the jungle region. Yet Christian faith shone through the ashes of burnt churches and homes.

Organized violence against Christians has been reported in several parts of the world at the dawn of the third millennium. China, Egypt, Indonesia, Iraq, Nigeria, North Korea, and Pakistan stand out among the countries that have witnessed severe persecution of the followers of Christ in recent times. The casualty figures in Kandhamal were lower than those in Nigeria or Iraq. But the diabolical violence in Kandhamal remains in many ways unique. Unlike in other regions where Christians were simply targeted for attack, the Hindu fundamentalists' goal in Kandhamal was not merely to harm the Christians or drive them out of the region. Their target was to force the Christians to renounce their faith and embrace Hinduism.

Thousands of Christians fled to the jungles in August 2008, seeking shelter before marauding Hindu mobs could lay hands on them. The anti-Christian pogrom began when Hindu fundamentalists issued a declaration: "Christianity is a foreign rligion, and only Hindus can live in Kandhamal." This announcement was an angry reaction to the murder of Swami Lakshmanananda, a fundamentalist leader. Swami Lakshmanananda had preached that Christianity must be banished from Kandhamal. When he was killed, his followers blamed Christians for the crime—wrongly. Soon the murder was traced to a Maoist group, but that fact did not change the behavior of the Hindu militants, who felt that they were carrying out the wishes of their slain leader by launching mob violence against Christians.

Dozens of defiant Christians who were caught by the roving Hindu mobs were tortured and brutally murdered. Hundreds of others were coerced to undergo a "reconversion" ceremony, made to drink cow-dung water to "purify" them, and recite dreadful oaths swearing that they would never return to the churches. This pogrom targeting Christians was carried out with clinical precision in village after village, with government officials turning a blind eye. The Hindu fundamentalists felt triumphant.

However, undaunted by the threats, many valiant Christians stood by their faith. Instead of returning to their villages to be "reconverted" into the Hindu fold, they preferred to languish in the squalor of refugee camps and urban slums as true followers of Christ. Even among the more than 2,000 Christians who underwent "reconversion" under death threats, most soon returned to their Christian faith.

The Orissa government, which was under the control of a Hindu nationalist party, virtually endorsed the anti-Christian campaign, shutting down the refugee camps and dumping homeless Christians near their villages, in desolate areas where they were at the mercy of the mobs. Still the Christians held firm in their faith—and even continued to bear witness by showing no ill will toward their tormenters.

While the orgy of violence went on for weeks, persecution of various kinds continued even after three years. Hundreds of Christians were languishing outside their villages even in 2012 as they were not prepared to meet Hindu fundamentalists' precondition for getting back their homes and normal lives—renouncing their faith.

The orchestrated violence in Kandhamal was the most painful episode in the history of Christianity in India. But it may also be the most glorious moment for Christianity in India since St. Thomas the apostle brought the faith to India in 52 AD. The unwavering witness of the Kandhamal Christians under brutal persecution has started melting even the hardened hearts of those who had tried to banish Christianity from the region. Stunned by the steadfast faith of the persecuted Christians, dozens of Hindus—including some who participated in the brutal assaults in 2008—have already flocked to the churches, as pagan Romans once did when they witnessed the steadfastness of the martyrs in the Colosseum.

Ironically, the Indian persecution is in one way worse than what happened in Rome; it occurred in a country that loudly proclaims the freedom of religion, and promises believers protection in its constitution.

## A Martyr's Village Becomes a Magnet of Faith

Two dozen Christians were dancing excitedly to the tune of hymns on a Sunday afternoon. It was New Year's Day 2012, in Gadragam village, and the celebration took place among the ashes where a disabled Christian youth named Rasanand Pradhan had been burned to death—the first Christian martyr in Kandhamal.

"When we realized that Rasanand was left behind, we could do nothing about it," recalls Rabindra Pradhan, the victim's elder brother. "The memory of the house going up in flames, with Rasanand inside, still haunts me." But the death of the young man has left another legacy, his brother said.

"Our people are no more afraid. They are ready to profess their faith boldly," said Rabindra. "The martyrdom of my brother has not gone waste. Half a dozen Hindu families are now regularly attending our worship," he continued. He proudly pointed out among the Christian crowd a retired Indian soldier who had have been moved to join the Church.

Kartick Behra, a Hindu who has been attending church service in the village for a year, observed: "We have been inspired by the faith of these people. So we decided to become Christians." Behra, a poor farmer, began coming to the church when he fell sick, and reports that the illness soon left him. He once considered Christians a threat; now he sees them as friends. "Many more (Hindu) families here now want to become Christians," said Behra, whose wife and four children also now attend church regularly.

Hippolitus Nayak, a retired government official and a Catholic, had a pleasant surprise on the the same New

Year's Day. Lakhno Pradhan, a local Hindu fundamentalist leaders, who had led mob attacks on Christians and churches around Tiangia, greeted him at his door with a flower.

"He apologised to me for what the Hindu mobs had done to the Christians," said Hippolitus cheerfully a few hours after the meeting, as he arrived at the rebuilt church for Mass. He added: "Many of the Hindus who used to keep away from us have started interacting with us now. Earlier they used to turn their faces away. There is certainly regret among them for the atrocities committed on us."

Nayak, whose own house had been destroyed in the anti-Christian violence, reported that several of the people now regularly attending Sunday Mass in Tiangia were among the Hindu witnesses to the brutal murder of several Christians who refused to renounce their faith.

"Coming to the church gives me peace of mind. Nothing is going to change my decision," said Jamboti Digal, while rushing to get to Sunday Mass. The widow from Gudribada village said that "seeing the faith of these people" had moved her to look into Christianity. Then she peeked in the church and saw that the liturgy was starting—and ended the interview.

Among the Hindus in Kandhamal who have been attracted to the Church after the violence, some were not only witnesses but participants. "I was forced to join the mob to destroy Christian houses and the church. After that, I felt that I had done something wrong and had no peace of mind," admitted Bony Pradhan. "Along with my wife, I decided to become a Christian."

## A Persecutor Becomes a Christian

Some more active persecutors tell similar stories. "We harassed them and destroyed their houses. But they have no hatred or anger against us," said Junos Digal, a member of the mob that attacked Christian targets. Squatting on a mat, with a Bible in front of him, he continued: "They are still suffering. But they have no complaints and they are living happily. There is certainly something special about how their faith enables them to overcome difficulties. This has brought me here. If Jesus could influence people's lives to such an extent, I would prefer to be a part of that faith," Digal said.

Asked whether he was worried that other Hindu fundamentalists would not turn their ire toward him for betraying their cause, Digal gave an interesting reply: "Many of us were misled. Now they will accept the reality. I am not worried about that." Junos's wife, Sailama, embraced Christian faith before he did. She said simply: "My conscience made me take this decision." She too is unworried about a possible angry reaction from militant Hindus. " God will protect us," she says. "If we live, we live for Christ and if we die, we die for Christ."

The entry of more than a dozen such new converts to their congregation brought joy and comfort to the

Christians who had held to their faith amid persecution. "In our suffering, our faith has been strengthened," said Jayanti Digal. "Even when we were suffering, our faith kept us going. Now we are glad that even those who attacked us have started embracing our faith," she said.

Rupara Digal, who had been the Hindu priest of nearby Puisaru village, joined with three other families to become Christian in June 2010. "One of them surrendered this axe here," said a Protestant pastor, showing the traditional wide-faced axe that is used for Hindu animal sacrifices. This axe, he added, had been used for generations—perhaps even for the human sacrifices that were prevalent in Kandhamal jungles long ago.

Similar sentiments were heard at Mokabali village. Sitting inside a mud-thatched church, Mithun Digal narrated how he along with his wife, with sixteen other Hindus of the village, embraced Christianity. "I have seen the violence and their suffering. Yet they have not given up their faith. So I decided to embrace their faith," reasoned Mithun.

Rajnikant Digal, another convert, said: "Fear of God is behind my change of faith." Despite their suffering, he found the Christians were happy and loving. "I wanted to experience the same joy," he added.

Rajnikant too found that local Christians were ready to accept him and his family despite what they had suffered. "We are happy now as we have more people to pray together," says Roopa Digal, an Evangelical Christian whose home was burned down and rebuilt in January 2010 with support from the Catholic Church. "This gives us greater confidence."

## Conversion Can Be Illegal

The Kandhamal government had assigned the major Christian denominations to coordinate the reconstruction of destroyed or damaged houses in the region. The Catholic Church took up the work in the areas of Raikia that were worst hit. During the distribution of building material, Church officials decided to reach out also to dozens of Hindu families of the *dalit* (lower caste) class whose houses had been damaged earlier.

"Many of them are coming to us, saying that they want to become Christians," reported Rev. Bijay Kumar Pradhan, who was coordinating the Catholic housing program. These Hindus were impressed by the concern the Christians had shown them. "Forgiveness has its effect," said Rev. Bijay. But he promptly added that he cautioned these Hindus that the Church was not rebuilding their houses to lure them into Christianity.

"We are happy that God is melting the hardened hearts in Kandhamal now," said Rev. Prabodh Kumar Pradhan, confirming that three prominent Hindus approached him with a request to be baptised. However Rev. Prabod, who took over as vicar of the Raikia parish in 2011, told them that one cannot become Christian overnight. He asked them to wait to see if they were serious about their decision to embrace Christianity. He also reminded them that they had to attend catechism classes before they could be baptized.

With Hindus applying to embrace the Christian faith all across Kandhamal, the clergy is treading cautiously. "We have to be careful as the law could put us in trouble," said Rev. Pradhan. "We also need to ensure that they are serious, and not laying a trap for us."

Under the Orissa Freedom of Religion Act, those changing their faith and religious leaders undertaking the conversion ceremony have to seek prior permission from the district executive. Accepting Hindus into the Church without this prior permission from government officials would make both the converts and the priests who welcomed them subject to prosecution.

## Playing by the Rules

The fire-scarred Capuchin seminary compound at Barakhama witnessed an unprecedented event on December 18, 2011. As many as sixty-four Hindus, belonging to thirteen families, including adults and children, were baptized in the singed hall of the seminary, with prior permission from government officials under the Orissa Freedom of Religion Act.

"We did not want the government officials to harass us later. So we told them (the converts) to inform and get (prior) permission from government officials before the baptism," explained Rev. Robi Sabhasundar, a priest of the Balliguda parish in which the Capuchin seminary is based. "It was a memorable event in the context of the violence."

"We have the freedom to choose our faith and we decided to exercise it to stop our persecution," said one of the newly baptized Christians, Jalandhar Digal, in July 2012. The converts came from Melsikia, a little village about five miles from Barakhama. For years these *dalits* had been living in Melsikia, side by side with over 150 other Hindu families. But the upper castes often treat the *dalits* as untouchables, and when the Hindu supremacists rose in anti-Christian violence, these *dalit* families also felt the pressure. Jalandhar Digal recalls being told: "You are not Hindus. We don't want you to live among us."

"They even destroyed our houses," Jalandhar says. "Since we were few in number, we could not challenge them." So the eighteen families built new homes in a forlorn forest area, where not even a mud road reaches their settlement. "All of us held a meeting and decided to become Christians," said Lupara, another convert. Of the eighteen *dalit* families, thirteen became Catholic while the other five joined a Pentecostal church.

Rev. Gregory Jena, superior of the Capuchin centre, said the intimidated *dalits* of Melsikia first established contact with a Catholic layman who was taking care of the forsaken Capuchin complex. When the Capuchin priests returned to the seminary, the contact became more regular. "We visited them frequently and started giving them catechism classes and conducting prayers with them. On feast days, they used to come (on bicycles) to Balliguda church to see how the Catholics practiced their faith. It was only after nearly two years of preparation, we decided to baptize them and insisted on getting the permission from the government."

But the road to conversion was not an easy one. The moment the Hindu Kandhos heard that the *dalits* were planning to embrace Christianity, persecution started anew. "Even the women prevented us from drawing water from the village well. They stopped employing us to work in their fields. They would not allow us to collect firewood from the forest in their area. Sometimes, they would threaten and even abuse us," Puninga Digal, a mother of two, said. The harassment eased only when the *dalits* lodged a complaint with local police.

Although the government officials in Balliguda were taken aback when the *dalit* families insisted on becoming Christians, the officials made no attempt to threaten or dissuade them.

## All Manner of Evil Against You

Hindu fundamentalists in Dakka village near Barakhama were incensed when Londo Mallick, the richest farmer of the area, embraced Christianity in July 2011. The tribal community of over 400 Hindu families had reason to be angry with the forty-five-year-old farmer. He had even destroyed the *puja* (worship) altar at which traditional animal sacrifices had been held for years—in the courtyard of his house, since as he headed the *puja* committee. "They were angry with me for becoming a Christian and suddenly stopped interacting with me," Mallick said in July 2012.

For Mallick the path to conversion began with a loss of faith in Hindu worship: "My wife Sakuntala was sick and I took up the responsibility of conducting the *puja* in the hope of her recovery thirteen years ago. But her condition only got worse over the years and she was on the verge of death. I heard about people getting healed in (Christian) prayer meetings. I took my wife to a three-day prayer meeting and Sakuntala got well all of a sudden in June (2011). Then we decided to become Christian."

The next month Mallick submitted to government officials a declaration that his family wished to change faith. "My conscience also pricked me as I had led the local Hindus to destroy Christian houses during the violence in 2008," he said. "During the prayers, I prayed for forgiveness, as I had also burnt Bibles during the violence."

With local Hindus imposing a "social boycott" against him and refusing to work in his fields, the only consolation for Mallick was the support of four Christian families in his village. He had endeared himself to these Christians during the violence as he had prevented the Hindu mobs from assaulting them and plundering their properties, since they had been trusted laborers on his farm for years.

Enraged over his leaving the Hindu fold, local Hindu fundamentalists were eagerly waiting for an opportunity to teach Mallick a lesson. A chance came their way when an eleven-year-old girl was accidentally killed by a friend who was cleaning a hunting rifle Mallick had lent to him. Half a dozen Hindu fundamentalists gave testimony to the police that the Christian convert had purposely lent the gun so that the man could kill the girl. The police arrested Mallick and charged him as a partner in the crime.

"While in jail, I prayed earnestly, and God worked a miracle. I was released after six days," said Mallick with his eyes gleaming. "We were all praying for him when he was in jail," said Nirmal Digal, who is himself a convert and now acts as a Pentecostal pastor. He arranged for a lawyer to defend Mallick, and soon the accused man was released.

While Hindu fundamentalists persisted with the "social boycott" against Mallick, some Hindus villagers secretly approached the bold convert seeking his advice on how they, too, could become Christian. Even before Mallick completed the first anniversary of his baptism, other villagers had begun attending prayer services in his house. "More Hindus will surely join us soon," said Mallick.

## Hearts Are Melting, One by One

Bamdev Kanhar was a typical Christian-baiter in Kandhamal. He had joined with armed mobs that were despatched by Hindu fundamentalist leaders to attack St. Peter's parish in Pobingia at Christmas in 2007. Since they could not lay hands on the parish priest, Rev. Prasanna Kumar Singh, they torched the church. Bamdev had even threatened local Hindus who had alerted the pastor, enabling him to flee in the nick of time.

Rev. Prasanna had to flee Kandhamal a second time in August 2008. Two months after his return, thirty-three-year-old Bamdev knocked on the door of the pastor's room in the night. Rev. Prasanna was taken back when he saw Bamdev at his door. Realising the tension on the face of the priest, Bamdev said: "Father, don't be afraid. I have come to apologize to you." The Hindu fundamentalist leader knelt before Rev. Prasanna and begged for pardon for the attack on the church.

"Bamdev has certainly undergone a change of heart and given up his aggressive attitude to the Christians," said Rev. Prasanna in July 2012. Months after the apology, Bamdev visited Rev. Prasanna again—this time openly, during daylight hours. He had brought a special papaya plant that yielded high-quality fruits and asked the priest to grow it in the church compound. Since he had received it from his hostile neighbour, Father Prasanna took extra care to nurture the plant. When Archbishop Cheenath visited the Pobingia parish in October 2010, Father Prasanna presented the "first fruit" from this special papaya plant to him and narrated the story behind it.

Touched by this tale, Archbishop Cheenath asked Father Prasanna to give a papaya from the same plant to

Bamdev. "He could not believe that, when I told him that the archbishop asked me to present him a papaya. Soon he was in tears," Father Prasanna recalled.

Sitting near the papaya tree that he had given to the church, Bamdev gave his own reflections: "I had been thinking a lot about the vandalization of the church. There were beautiful trees and plants around. We destroyed everything. Whatever happened here is wrong. I wanted to do penance for it. So, I gave the papaya plant to the church as symobol of my repentence."

Earlier Bamdev had proclaimed his remorse at a "peace meeting" of two dozen local Hindu and Christian leaders, convened by government officials to ward off a new outbreak of anti-Christian violence in the days leading up to Christmas in 2010. At this meeting, Bamdev surprised the Hindu fundamentalists present, urging them to mend their ways and to stop harassing the Christians. "God will punish those who commit the crime of attacking churches and Christians," Bamdev bluntly warned. However, Bamdev gave no hint at that meeting that his change of heart could be traced to the sudden death of a Hindu who had taken part in an earlier attack on St. Peter's church, in Christmas 2007.

On that occasion, after setting fires in the church, rectory, and an attached student hostel, some of the assailants climbed on top of the concrete roof of the church. They started chipping with metal cutters at the foot of the fifteen-foot high cross on the roof, saying that they could not tolerate the sight of a big cross standing on top of the church. As they chipped at the base, one of the hooligans scoffed at the cross: "Jesus, if you are God, why don't you come out instead of hiding inside the cross?"

The next evening, two of these same hooligans, who were brothers, had a drinking bout and began a quarrel. In a fit of rage, the younger brother stabbed the elder to death. The victim was the same young man who had mocked Jesus on the cross; the killer, his brother, was sentenced to life imprisonment. Bamdev was deeply affected by the murder. "God will punish those who desecrate holy places," he said. "Many Hindus here are talking about it."

Soon Bamdev was regularly visiting the restored church which he had helped to torch, bringing flowers and donations to the priest along with his own prayer intentions.

A few days before Christmas 2010, Bamdev stunned Rev. Prasanna with a question: "Father, are you afraid of inviting me for Christmas service?" That innocuous request made the priest's spine shiver, as Rev. Prasanna was reminded of his nightmare flight through the jungle to escape the mob that had attacked the church in Christmas 2007. Rev. Prasanna told Bamdev that only Christians attended the church services, and so he saw no point in inviting him. But the priest could not believe his eyes when he found Bamdev among the faithful in the offertory queue, holding in his hands a basket full of fruits and flowers, during the midnight Christmas service.

Now Bamdev is edging close to Catholicism. "I have a rosary with me," he says. "I wear it sometimes to the temple also, and pray with it through I do not know any formal Christian prayers. Holding the rosary in my hands, I pray often in the night for peace and goodwill in the world."

### 'God's own people'

"I can only say they are God's own people," remarked Archbishop John Barwa on New Year's Day 2012 during his pastoral visit to the troubled Kambhamal region. "God's plans are beyond our comprehension. What happened here was very painful. It was not a curse. It is turning out to be a blessing. God has also blessed me to be with these valiant people," said Archbishop Barwa, who took charge of the persecuted church in Kandhamal in April 2011.

Asked about the enormous reconstruction task that lies ahead of him—with hundreds of broken houses, churches and institutions lying unrepaired even after three years, Archbishop Barwa responded:

> When the Israelites were in the desert, God took care of them. We need not worry about anything. Our call is to remain faithful to God. That is what the Kandhamal people have done. Despite all their suffering, our people have held on to their faith.
>
> The bloodshed and the (number of) martyrs here may be less compared to those who died in

the Colosseum. But the number of Kandhamal Christians who have suffered for their faith remains very high.

The special fast-track courts that were set up in Kandhamal to try those accused of leading the anti-Christian violence have regularly been acquitting even those charged with brutal murders. But when asked whether the Church planned to strengthen its legal effort to ensure justicee for the victims and their families, the archbishop deflected the question. "We believe in nonviolence, forgiveness, and conversion of hearts," he said. "Punishment will not make one mend his ways."

"We firmly believe that God's message of love can melt the hardened hearts," explained Archbishop Barwa. "Forgiveness can change people."

*Anto Akkara is an award-winning journalist covering religious concerns in South Asia. His book,* Shining Faith in Kandhamal *(Asian Trading Corporation, 2009), offers many more such testimonies of faith on the part of valiant, persecuted Christians. This chapter is an extract from his forthcoming book,* Early Christians of the 21st Century.

CHAPTER NINE

# Witness Without Words: Evangelization Under Islam

*Rev. Fabian Bashir*

IN MUSLIM NATIONS AROUND the world (including the Middle Eastern country where I served as a pastor) Islam is the official state religion. Freedom of worship is permitted to Christians, and various formal and informal agreements are in place with Catholic, Orthodox, and a few Protestant churches to regulate the solemnization of marriages and the conduct of private schools. Attempts to make converts are forbidden, however, and conversion to Christianity is without exception illegal. The bishops are at pains to preserve the limited freedoms that the Church enjoys and they discourage any suggestion that departures from the civil law might occur. For that reason the country where this story took place will not be named and my own authorship is pseudonymous.

The greater number of Latin-rite Roman Catholics resident in this country are not Arabs but Asian domestic workers—mainly women—from Sri Lanka, Indonesia, and the Philippines. Most have Muslim employers, many of whom are suspicious of the Christian faith of their maids, cooks, and nannies, and who make it difficult for them to attend Mass. Because Friday serves as the Muslim "sabbath"—the only day many domestics are permitted time off—the Mass held on Friday is generally the best attended of the week. It is hard to exaggerate the witness value of these poorly paid women who, having only a few hours free time each month at their disposal, chose to spend a good portion of it in worship at Mass (not to mention the costly and vexatious travel from their homes or workplaces).

Almost all the Asian domestics working abroad contribute to the support of family members in their country of origin and send back a great part of their wages for this purpose. Many put up with indignities and injustices at the hands of their employers without complaint for their families' sake. In addition, many foreign workers are illegals, having entered the country on a tourist visa, only to take employment forbidden by the terms of their entry—and, of course, beneath the minimum wage. Even more than the legal aliens, such workers are subject to abusive treatment—sometimes denied wages, free days, or even egress from their quarters; often sexually importuned; occasionally beaten or underfed. They rarely report abuse to the police, frightened of the consequences of the discovery of their illicit residency status. They are, in short, perfect victims.

### He Gives Dignity to Slaves

In these circumstances the Church tries to help ill-treated workers find more just conditions, but her primary task and principal gift is spiritual: insisting that even in degrading situations, the human person has a dignity as a child of God. Pope Benedict, in his encyclical letter *Spe Salvi*, spoke to dignity in recounting the journey of the nineteenth-century Ugandan saint (and foreign worker) Josephine Bakhita:

> Up to that time [Josephine] had known only masters who despised and maltreated her, or at best considered her a useful slave. Now, however, she heard that there is a *"paron"* above all masters, the Lord of all lords, and that this Lord is good, goodness in person. She came to know that this Lord even knew her, that he had created her—that he actually loved her. She too was loved, and by none other than the supreme *"Paron,"* before whom all other masters are themselves no more than lowly servants. She was known and loved and she was awaited. What is more, this master had himself accepted the destiny of being flogged and now he was waiting for her "at the

Father's right hand." Now she had "hope"—no longer simply the modest hope of finding masters who would be less cruel, but the great hope: "I am definitively loved and whatever happens to me—I am awaited by this Love. And so my life is good." (3)

By a happy irony, many of these workers who had been lax or perfunctory Catholics in their home countries are re-evangelized by turning to the Church in circumstances of danger and distress, where they learn for the first time that the freedom for which Christ made us free (Gal 5:1) can be claimed—even relished—in the worst of earthly conditions.

The dimensions of a priest's pastoral work are partly a response to the concrete conditions in which his parishioners live and work. The overwhelming preponderance of women in the Christian population meant that marriages were few, but the appetites and attitudes of Muslim employers and boyfriends (compounded with the hardships of separation from family and homeland) resulted in a high number of births all the same. Here the rigid legal structure made for a very delicate situation. By civil law, the child of a Muslim and non-Muslim parent is deemed a Muslim; if the mother is a Christian not married to the Muslim father, the child is taken away and placed in a Muslim orphanage; and of course, it is illegal to baptize a Muslim. For this reason I frequently chose not to inquire about the paternity of a child brought by its mother for baptism, and left the fatherhood line blank in the baptismal registry. If the father be deemed *ignotus* (unknown), he is thus conceivably non-Muslim—so that the child could be baptized without contravening the law of the state, and its mother, on leaving the country for her homeland, could take her child with her. In at least one case a male Christian parishioner, unbeknownst to the pastor, falsely claimed paternity of an illegitimate child, precisely so that her mother could have her baptized without difficulty and bring her home when she left the country.

There are comparable difficulties in the (rarer) case of marriages. *Shari'a* law forbids a Christian man from marrying a Muslim woman—in this nation, without exception—but permits a Muslim man to marry a Christian woman. Any children of their union are perforce Muslims, and must remain Muslims even after the death of their father or in the event of divorce or abandonment. The parish included a number of women married at one time to Muslims, who comprised an informal support group, seeking advice on ways to deepen their faith in the face of their husband's ridicule or the hostility of their ex-husband's in-laws. Their children sometimes accompanied them to Mass and even received Christian religious instruction, but conversion to Christianity could only take place after emigration to a non-Islamic country, and would forfeit all rights of inheritance. Few had the gumption and wherewithal to make such a radical decision. For all that, the parish contained a number of these "ghost Christians" who prayed, studied, and gave alms as Catholics—though without receiving the sacraments—yet who remained officially Muslim. In this connection we can remember Naaman the Syrian (2 Kgs 5:18) who asked pardon of the Lord for bowing his head in the Temple of Rimmon when accompanying his master the king. Many who are not yet ready to face persecution are doing the best that they can.

## The Grim Face of Repression

In spite of the strict rules against preaching and conversion, there are many citizens, including Muslims, who approach the Catholic Church to ask for baptism. The fact of the matter is that there is a ceaseless "evangelization of over-hearing." Catholics have the liberty to instruct one another in the faith by means of television and radio programs, and have used this opportunity to great advantage, with extensive Arabic-language programming in all forms of media. While the intended audience of such programming is those already baptized, the *de facto* audience is nonetheless entirely unrestricted: many Muslims listen in. It goes without saying that the Internet has made national boundaries entirely porous and controls on speech greatly enfeebled, with the consequence that almost any person inclined to listen to the Christian message is able to do so. Of course such self-instruction at second hand lacks the full human impact of person-to-person testimony, but, as St. Augustine insisted, *bonum est diffusivum sui*: that which is good communicates itself, and replicates itself in the telling. The Gospel cannot be chained, and in the face of all obstacles ceaselessly pulls new hearers to the feet of Christ.

Once again, however, complications arise when the non-Christian accepts the Word and asks to enter the Church. If an illegal baptism comes to the attention of the civil authorities, the bishop, by such a violation of the agreement with the state, risks losing the freedom to worship—not only that of Catholics, but other Christians as well; the same applies to licenses for Christian schools and media. Knowledgable converts from Islam claim that spies sometimes insert themselves in church services to hunt for apostates. Other indications of conversion, such as a Muslim's ceasing to attend services at his mosque or prayers at his workplace, can set in motion an intense level of government scrutiny into his life, with severe consequences. In addition, the convert almost always has to face hostility from the Muslim members of his family—hostility often so intense as to surpass the hardships threatened by Islamic officialdom. For these reasons, the bishop in almost every case will advise the Muslim catechumen to leave for a non-Islamic country, where he would be free to practice his Catholic faith.

Yet Muslim conversions to Catholicism are not negligible. In some few cases, the bishop will agree to a clandestine baptism in his own territory. More frequently, the convert will travel to another country for a brief period, undergo baptism, and then return without acknowledging his conversion except to a few trusted persons. Not surprisingly, these converts live their faith in the shadows, sometimes showing up for Mass late and leaving early, or climbing into the choir loft so as to worship out of sight. On the part of the priest, some of his most painful and difficult hours as a confessor involve time with a penitent trying to sort out sinful from permissible acts of evasion.

What if an employer confronts the new Christian with rumors of his conversion? Can he in good conscience exchange greetings that imply he is still a Muslim? Can he join in the *adhan*—the Islamic "call to prayer"—while at his workplace or in the classroom? Can he absent himself from Mass on holy days if church-going would tip off the authorities? All the thorny and abstruse cases of conscience that tormented English Catholics in penal times are vividly present to these converts, with the added knife in the vitals provided by the fear that, in letting oneself be acknowledged as a Muslim, one is not only letting down the Church (as the Catholic who feigned Protestantism might do), but denying Christ. It is a dreadful business.

## Reinventing the Early Church

Muslim converts share with the Asian guest-workers the problem of the Christian education of their children. For most guest-workers, the fees charged by the Christian schools are prohibitive; for the converts, sending their children to Christian schools would tip off their change of religion. The state-run schools are free, but inculcate Islam to all students. As a consequence, the parents in both cases must take upon themselves their children's instruction in the faith, aided where possible by the clergy and sympathetic, discreet laity. The results are sometimes disappointing, but surprisingly often these children respond to the seriousness of the situation and apply themselves to their catechism with an earnestness rare in their Western counterparts. The children of converts seem to grasp, at least intuitively, that what takes place in this after-hours education may be officially viewed as an act of subversion, that they are complicit in a risky endeavor. Because of this, the formulaic affirmations of belief that North American children can find tiresome take on a personal importance. Like home-schoolers in other countries, parents they must attempt to master the material they wish to transmit, with the result that their understanding of doctrine is deeper and more accurate than those whose religious instruction ended with their youth. As with any underground association, the riskier one's loyalties, the more precious they become.

The Middle East today recalls the predicament of new Christians in the Roman Empire. When we consider the addressees of the epistles of St. Paul, for example, we realize that the congregations he instructed were composed largely of artisans, maids, tavern attendants, shopkeepers—living and working as a tiny minority in a civilization that capriciously alternated between tolerance and hostility. Their faith was something they needed to learn "on the job," while discreetly passing on to others the truths only recently learned. The preaching of the Good News oscillated between boldness and caution, and circumstances such as official rigor, family jealousy, and the presence of paid informers hampered freedom and increased the cost of discipleship. So also today, Christians living in Muslim countries have not ceased to evangelize, but their work skates two sides of a knife: a visible Church that tends to her own members with the grudging permission of the state, and an underground Church of curtained windows and lowered voices that quietly seeks out new souls.

As in every place and time, the most eloquent testimony to the Gospel is the lives of those who profess it. The Archbishop of Paris, Cardinal Emmanuel Suhard, said to his priests in the 1940s: "To be a witness does not consist in engaging in propaganda, nor even in stirring people up, but in being a living mystery. It means to live in such a way that one's life would not make sense if God did not exist."

The choices made by Catholics living in the Middle East make no sense in a God-less world. So they bear striking witness to the faith. As I have suggested, these Catholics are not angels but sinners—often public sinners—and many on occasion have submitted under pressure to less than noble compromises with the forces of state and society. Yet for all that they continually renew their contrition and ask forgiveness, and stubbornly persist in recourse to the Church and her sacraments.

There is an elementary moral beauty to these unimportant, unregarded persons making a simple act of humility which is, politically and religiously, an act of defiance. One of the images that remains in my mind concerns a fluke winter storm, with diminutive Asian women—underpaid nurses and over-burdened housekeepers—shivering beside the curb after Mass in the blowing sleet, as taxis filled with warm and wealthy Arabs passed them by. Everyone knows how little free time is allotted these women and how little money they have to hand. Everyone realizes that, in preference to coming to Mass, they might have spent these hours sleeping or shopping or recreating with friends. Everyone understands, even if the words are lacking, that they are hungry for the Bread of Life. Witness is borne. The Good News is preached.

*Fabian Bashir is a pseudonym for a former pastor to Latin-rite Catholics in a Muslim country.*

**CHAPTER TEN**

# "For I Languish with Love": Filling Up Those Empty Confessionals

## J. J. Ziegler

THE ELEVENTH POEM in the *New Oxford Book of English Verse* is a medieval lyric entitled *"Quia Amore Langueo"* ("For I Languish with Love"). It begins:

> IN the vale of restless mind
> I sought in mountain and in mead,
> Trusting a true love for to find,
> Upon an hill then took I heed;
> A voice I heard (and near I yede)
> In great dolour complaining tho:
> See, dear soul, how my sides bleed:
> *Quia amore langueo.*[1]

The Latin words come from the second chapter of the Song of Songs, and the sorrowful voice is that of Jesus Christ, who suffers in body, and even more in heart, because of the infidelity of the members of his spouse, the Church:

> Upon this hill I found a tree;
> Under this tree a man sitting;
> From head to foot wounded was he,
> His hearte blood I saw bleeding.
> A seemly man to be a king
> A gracious face to look unto.
> I asked how he had paining:
> > [He said]: *Quia amore langueo*
>
> I crowned her with bliss, and she me with thorn;
> I led her to chamber, and she me to die;
> I brought her to worship, and she me to scorn;
> I did her reverence, and she me villainy.
> To love that loveth is no maistry:
> Her hate made never my love her foe:
> Ask me then no mo questions why—
> > *Quia amore langueo.*

Although much has changed in the six centuries since the writing of the poem, it still speaks to Christians today. However far our culture may have drifted from Jesus

Christ, most Americans still have a warm, positive feeling about him; and then by grace we begin to understand that he has more than just a warm, positive feeling about us. We begin to understand, in the words of St. Paul, that "He loved me and gave himself for me" (Gal 2:20); we begin to understand, in the words of Pope Benedict XVI, that "we are not some casual and meaningless product of evolution. Each of us is the result of a thought of God. Each of us is willed, each of us is loved, each of us is necessary. There is nothing more beautiful than to be surprised by the Gospel, by the encounter with Christ."[2]

As we respond to the love of Christ, it dawns on us as well that his foundational teaching is neither "be nice" nor "I'm OK, you're OK," but "repent, and believe in the Gospel" (Mark 1:15). When Jesus sent out his apostles two by two, "they went out and preached that men should repent" (Mark 1:15). When St. Peter spoke to thousands on the day of Pentecost, he told his hearers that they should "repent, and be baptized every one of you in the name of Jesus Christ for the forgiveness of sins" (Acts 2:37–38). The message of repentance was not limited to the unbaptized; some two dozen years later, St. Paul pleaded with the baptized Christians of Corinth to "be reconciled to God" (2 Cor 5:21).

In seeking to repent, to be reconciled to God, we begin to understand (like the speaker in the poem) that we have not broken arbitrary dictates but have wounded the heart of Christ, who teaches that the proof of our love for Him is obedience to his commandments. "You are my friends if you do what I command you" (John 15:13). He said the night before he died; and St. John taught that "by this we may be sure that we know Him, if we keep his commandments. He who says 'I know Him' but disobeys his commandments is a liar" (1 John 2:3–4).

In repenting, we find that our love is mingled with fear, for we know that Jesus taught in the Sermon on the Mount that "the gate is wide and the way is easy, that leads to destruction, and those who enter by it are many" (Matt 7:13). Jesus Christ spoke often of the reality of hell, taught that obedience to the Decalogue is necessary for eternal salvation (Matt 19:17–20), cautioned that deliberate sins of lust and anger merit hell (Matt 5:22, 28–29), and warned that those who ignore the needy will receive an eternal punishment of fire (Matt 25:41–46). Certain sins, St. Paul taught, exclude one from the kingdom of God (1 Cor 6:9–10); certain sins, St. John taught, are mortal (1 John 5:16–17). Christians who "sin deliberately after receiving the knowledge of the truth," the author of the Letter to the Hebrews warned, face "a fearful prospect of judgment, and a fury of fire" (Heb 10:26–27).

These two thoughts—"I have wounded the heart of the incarnate God," and "I could spend eternity in hell"—can penetrate our minds by grace today, just as they penetrated the mind of the author of "*Quia Amore Langueo.*" The remedy for our sins is the same now as it was during the Hundred Years' War: the sacrament of penance and reconciliation, instituted by Christ on Easter evening, when he breathed on his apostles and said, "Receive the Holy Spirit. If you forgive the sins of any, they are forgiven, if you retain the sins of any, they are retained" (John 20:22–23).

Integral to this post-baptismal forgiveness, the apostles taught, is our confession of sins. St. John wrote that "if we confess our sins, he is faithful and just, and will forgive our sins and cleanse us from all unrighteousness" (1 John 1:8–9). This confession may be made not only to the apostles (and by extension to their successors, the bishops), but also to priests: St. James' admonition to "confess your sins to one another" (Jas 5:16) takes place in the context of his discussion of the anointing of the sick by the *presbyteroi* (presbyters, priests). In this confession to bishop or priest, the soul will find cleansing:

> In my side I have made her nest;
> Look in, how weet a wound is here!
> This is her chamber, here shall she rest,
> That she and I may sleep in fere.
> Here may she wash, if any filth were,
> Here is seat for all her woe;
> Come if she will, she shall have cheer,
>   *Quia amore langueo.*

## The Rise and Fall of a Sacrament's Use

"Over the centuries the concrete form in which the Church has exercised this power [of forgiveness] received from the Lord has varied considerably," according to the *Catechism of the Catholic Church* (1447). In time, the sacrament came to be "performed in secret between penitent and priest. This new practice envisioned the possibility of repetition and so opened the way to a regular frequenting of this sacrament. It allowed the forgiveness of grave sins and venial sins to be integrated into one sacramental celebration."

In 1215, the fathers of the Fourth Lateran Ecumenical Council enjoined Catholics to confess their sins annually (Canon 21), and in the Renaissance, the teaching Church was exhorting Catholics to go to confession frequently.[3]

Members of the clergy, called to be ambassadors of this authoritative teaching, have not always welcomed it. In 1786, the diocesan Synod of Pistoia (Italy) discouraged frequent confession, leading Pope Pius VI to condemn the synod's attitude as "rash, dangerous, contrary to the practice of the saints and the pious" (*Auctorem Fidei*, 1539). In 1943, Venerable Pius XII warned that "deplorable ruin...follows from the opinions of those who assert that little importance should be given to the frequent confession of venial sins.... Let those, therefore, among the younger clergy who make light of or lessen esteem for frequent confession realize that what they are doing is alien to the Spirit of Christ and disastrous for the Mystical Body of our Savior (*Mystici Corporis Christi*, 88).

Despite the opinions of these "younger clergy," the Second Vatican Council (1962–65) upheld the value of frequent confession (*Sacrosanctum Concilium,* 59) and exhorted priests to "show themselves altogether and always ready whenever the sacrament is reasonably sought by the faithful."[4]

Nonetheless, fewer Catholics in the United States frequented the confessional in the decades that followed the Council. The Notre Dame Study on Catholic Parish Life, conducted between 1982 and 1984, found that among "core Catholics"—that is, Catholics known to parish personnel—"27% never go to confession. . . . Another 35% go to confession once a year; 33%, several times a year; 5%, once a month; and 1%, more frequently than that."[5]

Lamenting the decline in the sacrament's use and wishing to make "reconciliation the center of the jubilee year called to celebrate the 1,950th anniversary of the redemption," Blessed John Paul II convened a synod of bishops in 1983 to discuss the theme of "Reconciliation and Penance in the Mission of the Church" (*Reconciliatio et Paenitentia,* 4 and note 8). In his post-synodal apostolic exhortation, the Pontiff stated bluntly that

> the sacrament of penance is in crisis. The synod took note of this crisis. . . . Meanwhile, from the synod itself the Church has received a clear confirmation of its faith regarding the sacrament which gives to every Christian and to the whole

community of believers the certainty of forgiveness through the power of the redeeming blood of Christ.

The pope concluded that the

> sacrament of confession is indeed being undermined, on the one hand by the obscuring of the [moral] and religious conscience, the lessening of a sense of sin, the distortion of the concept of repentance and the lack of effort to live an authentically Christian life. And on the other hand, it is being undermined by the sometimes widespread idea that one can obtain forgiveness directly from God, even in a habitual way, without approaching the sacrament of reconciliation. (28)

The doctrinal and pastoral teaching on the sacrament of penance in the post-synodal apostolic exhortation (1984), the authoritative teaching on the sacrament in the *Catechism of the Catholic Church* (1992, 1997), and Blessed John Paul's apostolic letter *Misericordia Dei* (2001) helped to dispel catechetical confusion about the sacrament—a confusion that manifested itself in an illicit overuse of general absolution and in a version of the "fundamental option" theory that denied the inherent grave sinfulness of certain acts.

Despite these magisterial efforts, the sacrament's use continued to decline in the United States. A new study conducted by the Center for Applied Research in the Apostolate found that in 2008, following up on the earlier survey for practice in the 1980s, found that 45 percent of Catholics said that they *never* go to confession; 30 percent confess less than once a year; 12 percent confess once a year; 12 percent confess several times a year; and only 2 percent confess once a month or more. Even among Catholics who attend Mass at least weekly, 15 percent said that they never go to confession; 23 percent confess less than once a year; 25 percent confess once a year; 31 percent confess several times a year; and only 6 percent confess once a month or more.[6]

Thus tens of millions of Catholics in the United States are failing, for whatever reason, to fulfill the second precept of the Church: "You shall confess your sins at least once a year."[7] Yet Jesus Christ still languishes with love for them, and the dozen years since the dawn of the third millennium have witnessed quiet initiatives in some two dozen dioceses encouraging them to return to the sacrament.

> If thou be foul, I shall make thee clean;
> If thou be sick, I shall thee heal,
> If thou mourn ought, I shall the mene;
> Why wilt thou not, fair love, with me deal?
> Foundest thou ever love so leeal?
> What wilt thou, soul, that I shall do?
> I may of unkindness thee appeal,
>   *Quia amore langueo.*

## Seeking God's Mercy

In his apostolic letter on preparation for the Jubilee in 2000, Blessed John Paul II stated that conversion would be one of the major themes of 1999, the year dedicated to God the Father. Conversion, he wrote, "is the proper context for a renewed appreciation and more intense celebration of the Sacrament of Penance in its most profound meaning" (*Tertio Millennio Adveniente*, 50).

The Archdiocese of Philadelphia, then led by Cardinal Anthony Bevilacqua, held an "intense celebration" of the sacrament on March 19-20, 1999, when an innovative "Reconciliation Weekend" took place in all 287 parishes as the culmination of a yearlong effort to help Catholics return to the practice of the sacraments. By offering indulgences in every diocese throughout the world during the Great Jubilee of the Year 2000—indulgences contingent upon confession and absolution—the Church again encouraged Catholics to return to the sacrament. During that year, the Archdiocese of Newark held a "Reconciliation Weekend," and every parish in the Diocese of Rockville Centre, the United States' sixth-largest diocese, began the tradition of offering confession during a common day and time in Lent.

"More than ten years ago, the Diocese of Rockville Centre began a practice of having priests available for the sacrament of confession and reconciliation in every parish of the diocese the Monday of Holy Week from 3 p.m. to 9 p.m.,"[8] Bishop William Murphy recalled in a 2011 diocesan newspaper column. "When I came here in 2001 I was deeply impressed by this extraordinary initiative that made it possible for so many to be absolved of their sins and so enter into the Holy Days of Holy Thursday, Good Friday, Easter Vigil and Sunday in the state of grace."

In 2007, the Archdiocese of Washington, under the direction of Donald Cardinal Wuerl, launched "The Light is ON for You" campaign, which has since become the most frequently replicated initiative promoting the sacrament. "Cardinal Wuerl, in talking with his priests, decided the archdiocese should focus on encouraging Catholics to return to the Sacrament of Reconciliation," recalled Susan Timoney, the assistant secretary of the archdiocese's Department of Pastoral Ministry and Social Concerns. "He chose the title of the initiative … and, after consulting with the archdiocesan priest council, decided the initiative would run in Lent, and that all 140 churches would be open at the same time every week during Lent (Wednesday evenings). The idea was to make it as easy as possible for people to come back." The campaign, conducted each year (with one exception) since 2007, has involved "hundreds of Metro and bus ads, radio ads, and a billboard."

Campaigns similar to Rockville Centre's (a lengthy opportunity for confession at the same time in every parish once during Lent) and Washington's (a common weekly confession time in every parish during Lent) have spread to other dioceses since 2007. Dioceses that have undertaken these or similar initiatives include the Archdioceses of Baltimore, Boston, Denver, Kansas City (Kansas), Miami, Mobile, New York, and St. Louis, and the Dioceses of Arlington, Baton Rouge, Bridgeport, Brooklyn, Fall River, Orlando, Paterson, Portland (Maine), Springfield (Massachusetts), St. Petersburg, Venice, and Worcester.

"I think like most dioceses we have seen a decline in the number of Catholics who avail themselves of the sacrament," said Ray Delisle, the Diocese of Worcester's vice chancellor of operations. "Like many things, if you get out of the habit of doing something good for yourself, body, mind, or soul, you may not get back into it. It is an example of the adage 'out of sight, out of mind.' Promoting the sacrament of penance and the healing graces it offers was done to bring it back into people's focus or attention, using public, secular media including radio and local TV, and reaching a variety of demographic groups by age."

The seal of confession limits information about these initiatives to scattered anecdotes from the laity and general impressions offered by priests and diocesan officials. Representative are the thoughts of the Father T. Kevin Corcoran, vice chancellor of the Diocese of Paterson: "It has been a great success. With a few exceptions, the priests say that it has made a big difference."

Washington's Susan Timoney and Worcester's Ray Delisle concurred. Timoney said that "the results since that first year in 2007 continue to be phenomenal. Each year we have done it, we have received such positive feedback from those going to confession and the priests in our parishes." Delisle observed, "Clearly every priest was seeing an increase in the number of people coming to avail themselves of the sacrament." Delisle added that anecdotal information "was most compelling: hearing about people who had been away from the sacrament for years and how moved they were by the experience of returning."

"People have come to confession that had been away for thirty, forty, or more years," said Timoney. "A man who had been away from the Church for twenty years, but whose wife was in RCIA, drove past the billboard every day for a month. On Holy Thursday, he went to Confession and at the Easter Vigil, joined his wife for her First Communion."

Dioceses have typically not publicized the numbers of penitents, though the Archdiocese of Philadelphia stated in a 2000 press release that "it is estimated that more than 100,000 people went to confession Reconciliation Weekend, including many who had not participated in the Sacrament of Reconciliation in years."[9]

New dioceses have begun to offer such initiatives each year; for instance, the Archdiocese of Denver's parishes first shared a common confession time on February 29, 2012. Bishop James Conley of Lincoln, then Denver's auxiliary bishop, called confession "the best kept secret of Catholicism," recalled Karna Swanson, the archdiocese's director of communications. "The Office of Communications promoted the event," Swanson added. "Our office had outdoor-quality banners printed. . . . We provided them to all of the parishes in the Archdiocese of Denver, and offered banners in Spanish also."

At times, dioceses have varied their approach: the Archdiocese of Philadelphia, which offered a Reconciliation Weekend under Cardinal Bevilacqua, has adopted an initiative similar to "The Light is ON for You" under the leadership of Cardinal Justin Rigali and Archbishop Charles Chaput.

While leading thousands of penitents to Christ's mercy, these initiatives have also affected the lives of the priests. "The priests have also been really touched by the experiences they have had," said Timoney, and some priests "expanded their confession schedule to include the lunch hour." Several priests of the Diocese of Paterson offered the following reflections on "Welcome to Healing," an initiative held on Lenten Mondays since 2009:

> I think that people are beginning to really appreciate the fact that they can go to another parish or church and heal old wounds. They like the fact that the priest does not know them and they are able therefore to come to the Lord with an open heart and mind.
>
> It was a real privilege for me to hear people's confessions on Monday night. Never did a night pass that I wasn't blown away by God's

loving plan in a person's life. He wants us to be in communion with him, and nothing but the hardness of our hearts can stop him!

I love hearing confessions, and so I looked forward to Monday nights to have such an opportunity. I was disappointed when I had very few penitents, but those that came really experienced all that the sacrament had to offer.... Some people came in upset, broken and feeling like they had the weight of the world upon their shoulders; however, when they left, it was amazing to see the transformation in the person. The sacrament is a very strong, albeit neglected sacrament that can benefit so many if people only knew and were not afraid to take advantage to experience the fullness of God's mercy. I saw it so many times and did everything I possibly could to lead them into the confessional: I preached about it, wrote about it in the bulletin, announced.[10]

In 2012, an initiative modeled on "The Light is ON for You" reached the shores of England. "We wanted a tangible and highly visible method of inviting people back to the Church and the life of the sacraments—the 'New Evangelization' in action," said Father Robert Billing, the bishop's secretary in the Diocese of Lancaster, who called the campaign "a deeply Catholic method that all the diocese could be involved in at the same time each week.

"Obviously, priests and people who have issues with confession, sin, 'institutional' aspects of [the] Church, etc., found the project difficult, but we expected this and continued on nonetheless with quite a significant degree of success," he mused. "Where priests swapped confessionals, where it was advertised properly by priests (using the Catholic schools), and where there was good and extra catechesis to our Mass-going people, there was notable success."

One or two other dioceses in England will follow suit and adopt the campaign, Father Billing predicted, and thus in the land of the author of *"Quia Amore Langueo,"* as in the United States, Christ will await the return of countless souls through these initiatives.

> I will abide till she be ready,
> I will her sue if she say nay;
> If she be retchless I will be ready,
> If she be dangerous I will her pray.
> If she weep, then bide I ne may;
> Mine arms bne spread to clip her me to.
> Cry once, I come. Now, soul, assay!
> *Quia amore langueo.*

*J. J. Ziegler, who holds degrees from Princeton University and the International Theological Institute (Austria), writes from North Carolina.*

## CHAPTER ELEVEN

# First Adore, Then Evangelize

### *Rev. Sean Davidson, MSE*

A*ND HE APPOINTED TWELVE, to be with Him, and to be sent out to preach.* (Mark 3:14)

Those disciples who were called to the first evangelization were first asked to "be with" the Lord, as this verse from the Gospel of St. Mark reminds us. This logic is of perennial validity for all those who seek to make Jesus Christ known and loved. We cannot give what we do not have, and so to make Christ known we must first know him personally. We do not have the privilege that the first apostles had of spending three years following the Son of God across the hills of Galilee and the highways of the Holy Land. Instead, we have the same Son of God, now enfleshed in the Most Blessed Sacrament.

*"Ave, verum corpus natum de Maria Virgine"* is the truth that generations have proclaimed in song while gazing upon the Host. The divine body hidden behind the humble white veil is indeed the same body of the Savior which was formed in the womb of the Blessed Virgin Mary all those centuries ago. The mystery of our faith assures us that the very same person who entered the world two thousand years ago still dwells among us. *Emmanuel* did not come to us for merely a passing moment but "always, to the close of the age" (Matt 28:20). It follows then that just as the apostles were called to first spend time with the Messiah before being sent out to announce his Gospel, all those who feel called to announce that same Gospel today should first of all spend time with the Holy Eucharist.

## The Eucharist: Source of Missionary Power

The great apostolic figures of our own times were conscious of the central place of adoration in the life of an evangelist and they lived in accordance with this truth. From the Venerable Archbishop Fulton Sheen, to Blessed Teresa of Calcutta, to Blessed John Paul II, those who succeeded in bringing Christ to the modern world first brought themselves to the Eucharist. The secretaries of Blessed John Paul tell us that before every missionary journey that pope would spend a prolonged period of time in front of the Blessed Sacrament. In spite of the busyness of his schedule he would often spend long hours, even in the middle of the night, prostrate before the Eucharistic Lord.[1]

A friend who worked at the apostolic nunciature in Paris once told me about one of Pope John Paul's visits there. The Holy Father arrived very tired exhausted—so thoroughly exhausted, in fact, that he had been unable to distribute Holy Communion during the Mass that morning. So when he arrived back at the nunciature at 12:45 p.m. everyone expected the pope to have a quick lunch, then retire to his room for a well-earned *siesta*. However the pope had "food to eat of which they did not know" (John 4:32). He entered the house and made straight for the chapel, while all those who were with him went directly to the dining room. They waited and waited for his arrival for lunch, but soon began to realize that for the Holy Father, lunch was off! Finally the pope emerged from the chapel at 4 p.m., having preferred to restore his strength by drinking from the fountain of divine grace for over three hours. Within minutes he was en route to the airport and back on his way to Rome, where an endless stack of letters and string of appointments awaited him.

It was because of his deep union with the Eucharistic Lord that Blessed John Paul II was such an indefatigable and transparent witness of Christ. As he would descend from the airplane in a new country, ready to pierce the darkness with the light of the Gospel, people were able to recognize in him a person who reflected the very light of Christ. Like Moses who descended the mountain of Sinai, still radiant from his encounter with the Lord, the Pope also seemed like one who "had been talking with God" (Exod 29:29). The light that emanated from his person was the light of the Eucharistic Face of Jesus. The words with which he touched so many hearts were a fruit of his long hours spent drawing inspiration from Jesus. Much of his writing was done during those long hours of Eucharistic adoration. Archbishop Fulton Sheen, who had a similar capacity to touch hearts, was fond of saying that he received this grace during his daily holy hour—or what he came to refer to as his "power hour."[2]

## From the Tabernacle to the Public Square

I belong to a small, new community based in France, the Missionaries of the Most Holy Eucharist, a community which seeks to establish Eucharistic adoration in parishes. Among our other tasks, we recruit and form volunteeers, and teach them the practicalities involved in maintaining this beautiful chain of uninterrupted prayer.

In my own journey to the priesthood it was discovering Jesus in the Eucharist which proved pivotal. I made my first official holy hour in summer 2003 and only fourteen months later, in August 2004, I entered the seminary.

After my conversion to Jesus Christ in 2000 I began to go to Mass every Sunday and then slowly but surely I began to go more and more frequently. Before long I had been observed by those who organized the perpetual adoration which has been going on unceasingly in my home town for almost thirty years. They invited me to come and spend one hour per week in front of the Blessed Sacrament in the little chapel next to the cathedral. As a wayward youth I had walked past this chapel almost every day, totally oblivious to the fact that behind that large brown door dwelled the King of Kings, along with the little court of faithful adorers who keep watch before him day and night. However the King was not indifferent to me. Little by little he was arranging everything for the day on which this lost sheep would find his way back to safety. In the end a series of events brought me to my knees in prayer in the year 2000, and coupled with the timely intervention of the Mother of God, who sent me some members of the Legion of Mary, the grace of my conversion was swiftly brought about.

So my Eucharistic adoration began in 2003 and continued to grow more and more intense over the coming months and years. Although not yet able to grasp the doctrine of the Real Presence, I was aware that in that chapel I felt peace. A weekly holy hour gave rise to a daily visit and before long a daily holy hour. The call to the priesthood, which had begun to manifest itself ever so gently the year before, soon became a persistent whisper and before long a clear calling. After having entrusted myself to Our Lady in the sanctuary of Knock in Ireland, I could soon no longer doubt my priestly vocation. With Mary's help and her rosary passing ever more frequently through my fingertips, inner resistance to the call soon gave way to joy and a deep to desire to leave everything for the glory of Jesus Christ. And so in 2004 the adventure officially got underway which would lead me to ordination on the Solemnity of Corpus Christi in 2011.

Once in seminary I discovered the little book entitled *The True Devotion to Mary* written by St. Louis-Marie de Montfort. As soon as my solemn consecration to Mary was accomplished, I could distinctly notice my prayer life change for the better. Longer periods in thanksgiving after Holy Communion ensued, as well as an ever more intense attraction to the light of the monstrance. In union with Our Lady I began to experience the reality of the Eucharistic presence ever more powerfully. I remember one evening in particular, as I made my way to the chapel for adoration, I asked Our Lady to teach me. As I entered the chapel that evening I had what I once heard described as the "shock" of the Real Presence. As I prostrated myself on the chapel floor in adoration of the Sacred Host, I could barely raise my eyes again. I was penetrated with a sudden sense of holy awe. I understood that upon that altar was present the One who walked the face of the earth 2000 years ago, who worked wonders, who was nailed to the Cross, and who rose again victorious from the tomb. By now I had come to understand what the Church teaches about the Eucharist. This truth I had accepted with my mind but on that evening it pierced my heart and it was as though I experienced it with every fiber of my being. My soul was flooded with joy as I gazed upon that host, rapt with wonder. The second person of the Blessed Trinity was in front of my eyes and his presence was nothing but love, pure and powerful love! The Woman of the Eucharist had given me the correct attitude to have in the presence of God Incarnate: what Pope John Paul II once called "Eucharistic Amazement" (*Ecclesia de Eucharistia*, 6). This experience renewed my manner of approaching the chapel and especially of receiving Holy Communion. I could no longer pass a chapel without entering to greet the Lord and prostrate myself before him. I would sometimes awake early in the morning with a thrill of joy as I realized that downstairs in the chapel the Son of God himself awaited me.

At this time, when the Eucharist began to take the central place in my life and as I began to spend long hours in adoration before the monstrance, another development began. I was aware of having a new grace for evangelization. I couldn't help but speak about Christ and my experience of his love to the people I would encounter in university lectures or on visits to my home town. I would write letters to my old friends telling them how they too might find their way out of the darkness into God's wonderful light. I do not want to exaggerate and pretend that I became like St. Francis Xavier overnight, but my experience of Eucharistic adoration very naturally led me to a renewed zeal for evangelization. And the people to whom I would speak were given the graces to listen.

Even I though I had often tried to evangelize before I hadn't had much success. It was only when I began to prolong my adoration and live with the joyful consciousness that Jesus Christ himself is alive and active in the Blessed Sacrament that my evangelization became effective. Many of my family members and closest friends soon came back to the sacraments, not just because of my words, but above all because of my intercession for them before the face of Christ. In order to evangelize effectively we must first obtain the grace in prayer. "Unless the Lord builds the house, those who build it labour in vain. . . . " (Ps 127:1). To bring souls to Christ, the Lord must inspire our words and he must also work in the heart of the person to whom we speak.

## Eucharistic Apostles

In the first chapter of the Gospel of John we read about the call of the first apostles. It begins with the prophetic evangelization of St. John the Baptist, who points out the presence of the Lamb of God. Immediately two of his disciples walk away from John and become the first of the apostles to follow Christ. Immediately after their first "holy hour" with Jesus, one of the young men, named Andrew, runs to share his joy with his brother Simon. His evangelization is immediate and filled with conviction: "We have found the Messiah!" (John 1:41). So powerful is this proclamation that Simon has no doubts. He runs with his brother to meet Jesus and immediately receives from Him a new name: *"Cephas"* or Peter, the solid rock upon which the Indestructible Church of God will be built. In other words, when Peter steps into the real presence of Christ he receives a new and most extraordinary vocation. By his apostolic labors Peter will go on to bring thousands of souls to the Lord and eventually he will give his life, which itself will become the seed of conversion for countless others. Starting from the powerful proclamation of St. John the Baptist, we have seen the beginning of a series of radical and almost immediate transformations. Those who spend time in the presence of Christ cannot help but bring others to him and those who come to Christ receive a mission from him; they go on to become instruments of evangelization and transformation.

This mystery of grace is still at work all over the world. Just as Andrew and John were able to go "and stay with him that day" (John 1:39), we are still able to go and "stay" with Christ thanks to the gift of perpetual Eucharistic adoration. It is as though we were on the hills of Galilee once again. The discovery of the Eucharistic Christ starts a chain reaction of radical transformations, similar to those we see in the Gospel, and God only knows what the end result of this powerful chain of grace will be for the Church.

## The Eucharistic Springtime

The perpetual adoration chapels which have multiplied in the last three decades are proving to be the power sources of the New Evangelization. When parishes begin to offer adoration, their efforts to evangelize begin to bear lasting fruit. I have had the privilege of helping to train adorers in many different countries and have been able to see that the transformation I enjoyed in own life is happening in chapels from one corner of the world to the other. From the rising of the sun to its setting, the Eucharistic Lord is at work to form apostles.

To borrow an image from Pope Benedict we are beginning to see a "Eucharistic Springtime" in the Church.[3] We might otherwise call it the "triumph of the Immaculate Heart of Mary," since Eucharistic adorers almost always claim that they received this grace through the mediation of Our Blessed Lady. After the long hard "Eucharistic winter," which was caused by a serious misinterpretation of the Second Vatican Council, we are now beginning to behold the first buds of this springtime.

Even in nature as winter is about to give way to springtime, the earth often appears to be still lifeless and barren. All we can see is the dark frostbitten earth of the winter months, but below the surface there is in reality an abundance of life. The little bulbs are already filled with life and are waiting to come forth and give to the world a magnificent array of springtime flowers. Similarly, as adoration chapels are coming into existence across the face of the earth, an abundance of spiritual life and holiness is taking shape and even beginning to blossom in many parts of the world. The saints of the third millennium are already being forged in the blazing furnace of Christ's heart and it will be these saints of the Eucharist who will lead the way.

To highlight the power of adoration in people's lives, I could recount many powerful stories which I have heard from adorers all over the world. But since space is limited, I will share just two, of people whom I know personally:

A friend of mine comes from Northern Ireland and was raised in a non-practicing Catholic family, which had been deeply affected by the political conflicts there. By twenty, after he had already found himself in serious trouble, a relative invited him to a retreat at a Marian sanctuary. After the first few days he was surprisingly content in this holy place, but had no real understanding of Catholic devotion to the Mass and the Eucharist. Then on the fourth or fifth day of the weeklong pilgrimage, the young man was standing among four of his friends and a total stranger walked up to them and said: "Do you want me to show you the quickest way to get to heaven?" He replied that he did, while his friends remained silent. The man said: "Then follow me." He was the only one to rise, and the man led him to the adoration chapel where he prostrated himself before the Blessed Sacrament. The young man looked down at this stranger who was now lying with his face flat on the floor and then looked back up at the Blessed Sacrament and perceived in his soul that this was not "something" but rather "some*body*," a human face with a gaze that pierced the depths of his soul. He prostrated himself in imitation of the stranger and when he walked out of that chapel, not only did he now have the gift of Catholic faith, but also the seeds of a vocation to be a Eucharistic apostle. He returned to Northern Ireland, started to adore every day and after hearing the Gospel in which Christ says: "Let the children come to me" (Mark 10:14), he began to bring the grace of adoration to children in local primary schools. He has recently decided to live a life of consecrated celibacy for the glory of the Blessed Sacrament.

The second story involves my childhood friend Rachel. Around the time of my conversion we began to drift apart. When I was in my second year of seminary, on the feast of the Conversion of St. Paul, God's providence arranged for our paths to cross once again. Immediately I began to encourage her to think about the Lord and her need for Him. We spoke for hours about Jesus, the mysteries of faith, and the power of the sacraments. Her heart was open and she was about as receptive to the grace of the Lord as any soul can be. Soon she was back at daily Mass, doing retreats and pilgrimages, and beginning to evangelize her own friends and family members. Before long she had consecrated herself to Mary and was spending several hours per day before the monstrance. With the extraordinary grace that she received from the Lord, Rachel managed to bring a large number of people back to the Church. One of these people in particular—who through her had come back to the sacraments after many decades—died suddenly only a few months later. (Thanks be to God this person had come back to the Lord and could leave this world in peace!) Since then I have been amazed by the success of Rachel's evangelization and her ability to reach souls who were once very far from the light of Christ.

Rachel has also shared with me many other wonderful things that the Lord has been doing through her to enkindle a veritable Eucharistic fire and to help bring about the renewal of the local Church. It seems that every single one of the four or five hundred faithful adorers at her chapel in Sligo could recount some story which shows the transforming power of adoration in their lives; and when we consider that there are more than 1,000 perpetual adoration chapels in the world, we can rejoice in the fact that there are hundreds of thousands of people receiving these extraordinary graces, week in and week out.

Along with the individual adorers who have become missionaries, there have also arisen many new movements, associations, and congregations, which trace their origin to the Eucharist. Wonderful groups, such as Youth 2000, which started in the United Kingdom, are bringing thousands of young men and women to recognize the Eucharistic Lord and to share this good news with their peers. In France, the Emmanuel Community, which has played a central role in the renewal of the Church in that country, roots its spiritual life firmly in the practice of daily Eucharistic adoration. In Italy *Nuovi Orizzonti* is engaged in constant Eucharistic evangelization of those furthest from the Lord. Nightfever in Germany is bringing souls straight from the street to encounter the hidden presence of Jesus in the Eucharist. Through the community *Eucharistein* in Switzerland the Lord is healing many tormented souls. In many different countries *Cenacolo* is bringing liberation to people suffering from addictions by exposing them to adoration, the holy rosary, and hard work. These young men and women are then becoming instruments of healing to others who have the same problems. New Eucharistic religious congregations, such as the Dominican Sisters of Mary Mother of the Eucharist in the United States, are teeming with vocations and helping to conquer a new generation of young people for Christ. The list of new movements and associations that have been born from the Eucharistic Heart of Jesus is a lengthy one, and bears witness to the direction that the authentic re-evangelization of humanity will take. As Pope John Paul II once said the Eucharist will be the root and center of the New Evangelization.[4]

## The Radical Transformation of the World

In addition to these visible transformations in the lives of adorers, there is also the hidden spiritual work of Jesus. Our adoration unleashes God's grace in just the same way that the faith of those people Christ encountered in the Gospels called up his miraculous power. As St. Peter-Julian Eymard would say in his conferences on adoration: "Eucharistic prayer has an additional merit: it goes straight to the Heart of God like a flaming dart; it makes Jesus work, act, and relive in his Sacrament; it releases his power."⁵ When we kneel before the Lord, we might say that Christ himself is "evangelizing." In her private apparitions, St. Faustina famously saw the two transforming rays of Christ's merciful power shooting forth from the host in the monstrance and touching an innumerable multitude of souls. Blessed Dina Belanger was given the grace to watch as souls were literally being preserved from eternal damnation because of her Eucharistic adoration.⁶ Once, when I was engaged in adoration in the middle of night, my heart was moved to pray for an old friend I hadn't seen in many years who was struggling with addictions. The next day I found out that at the exact time I felt moved to pray for him, he had been dying.

The fruits of our adoration will for the most part remain hidden to us until the Last Judgment, but occasionally Jesus gives us little glimpses of his Eucharistic power in order to encourage us to persevere in times of aridity. A priest in my own community once told me that a few years ago on the feast of St. Jean Eudes, he was spending a few hours before the Lord when he had the clear perception that Jesus was doing something very powerful at that moment, working in someone a powerful change of heart. My brother priest never forgot this powerful experience and continued to wonder what it was all about.

About one year later, a young man from the very same town as this priest, but unknown to him, descended from the plane in Marseilles airport and made his way to our community's base to begin his formation as a priest.

Everybody in the community was impressed by this young man's holiness and the long hours he would spend in deep recollection before the Blessed Sacrament. Shortly after his arrival, the community sat down to a pizza while the young man began to recount his conversion story. He had been very far from the Lord for several years but slowly began to make his way back. Then, just one year prior to his arrival in France, he was invited on a weeklong pilgrimage to a Marian shrine. One morning the young man was attending Mass, and just as the priest began to preach on the Gospel, the young man's heart was pierced by an extraordinary grace. He saw clearly that Christ was calling him to preach to a multitude of souls and that like the apostles he would have to leave everything behind for the glory of the Lord. In spite of the difficulties, he offered no resistance, and within weeks he had broken up with his fiancée and left his job in order to discern the will of the Lord. Soon he had absolutely no doubt that he was called to be a priest, with a special focus on devotion the Eucharist. As he finished the story, somebody asked him about the date on which his conversion had taken place and the young man casually responded: it was August 19. My priest friend almost choked on his pizza—that was the exact same day and same year that he'd had the intuition that Christ was changing someone's life.

Another young woman that I now arrived in France from Algeria, having been raised in an extremely strict Muslim family. One morning as the bells of the local church were ringing she felt an irresistible attraction to the sound. As she walked into the church, she saw a group of people on their knees before a "golden object" on the altar. Then quite suddenly she received an infusion of grace and saw with the eye of her mind that upon that altar was present the Lord and Savior of the world. All she could do was fall to her knees and adore. Soon she was giving her testimony before hundreds of young people, trying to make them understand the extraordinary privilege it is to be Catholic and to have the living presence of Jesus Christ in the Eucharist.

A priest who started perpetual adoration in a large town in Brittany began to see powerful changes all around him after adoration began. At first he was wary of having adoration through the night because it was a dangerous neighborhood. The church was situated on the street which was the center of prostitution for the entire city, and right in front of the church drugs were constantly being sold. However the pastor received what he believed was a sign that he should proceed. He felt obliged to ask the local police if they would be able to keep an eye on the adoration chapel and come immediately if ever there was a problem. The chief responded that he used to do adoration himself in Paris and that if the chapel was established not only would he keep an eye on it but he would also go there to adore. The perpetual adoration began and the pastor noticed an immediate change in the spiritual environment. Only one year later the neighborhood's criminal network was destroyed and drug dealing in the neighbourhood had stopped. Soon thereafter the prostitutes also decided to move on. The neighborhood is now one of the most sought-after locations in the city, with house prices rising considerably. The local real estate brokers have no idea what was the source of this rapid transformation, but the pastor is in no doubt.

Pope John Paul II once said that the person who prays in adoration contributes mysteriously to the "radical transformation of the world."[7] However it is important to note that we shouldn't engage in adoration merely as an instrument, to help us win people over. We should adore first of all because Christ is there and his perpetual loving presence merits a response of love. In his generosity Jesus will indeed do great things through our adoration, but even if he chose not to, he would still merit our love and our presence. Paradoxically it is the souls who come to Christ with this kind of pure gratuitous love who become the most successful and powerful evangelizers in the world.

## Imitating the Master

In many Gospel texts, Jesus himself shows us how to proclaim the Good News. Much is written about Christ's "Sermon on the Mount" but not enough is said about what immediately preceded this outpouring of divine wisdom. St. Luke tells us clearly that as a preparation, Jesus "went out to the mountain to pray; and all night he continued in prayer to God" (Luke 6:12). Nocturnal adoration is not something the Church has invented; it was the way that the Master himself prepared for his sermons and other important moments in his life! Nocturnal adoration was often practiced by great missionary souls such as St. Francis Xavier, whose words attracted thousands of souls to Christ. His days were spent preaching and many of his nights before the Blessed Sacrament.

Returning to the text from Luke, we see that after this long night of drawing power from the bosom of the Father, Jesus then comes back to cast fire upon the earth. Luke tells us that he "stood on a level place, with a great crowd of his disciples and a great multitude of people from all Judea and Jerusalem and the seacoast of Tyre and Sidon, who came to hear him...." (Luke 6:17). His holiness has drawn the multitudes, whom he will bless with the gift of divine insight. Christ's words turn the proud wisdom of the world upon its head and leave the open human mind fascinated. If the Church would begin to live in relation to the Blessed Sacrament the way that Christ lived in relation to the Father, our words too would become inspired words of light and wisdom to attract the world.

In this passage of Scripture, the holiness of Christ's presence drove the evil spirits out of people and cured many of their diseases "for power came forth from him and healed them all" (Luke 6:19). If we too would spend our nights exposing our souls to the light of the Lamb of God, then we would begin to be radiant with his holiness. Saints like Jean-Baptiste-Marie Vianney and Martin de Porres were known for their nocturnal and early morning adoration of the Blessed Sacrament and this is why their very physical presence was an exorcism of sin and a source of healing for the afflicted. Their bodies which were so often before the Lord in adoration had begun to reflect the properties of the sacred body of Jesus. Such adoration could make individual Catholics the instruments of salvation.

The third and final fruit of Christ's all-night vigil, which St. Luke points out, is the calling of the twelve apostles. Jesus after a night of loving consultation with the Father returns to his brothers and reveals which ones have been chosen to be at the forefront of the mission for the conversion of the world. Vocations are a gift from God and they are a fruit of prayer; they are obtained from the Lord when we kneel in humble supplication before him. This is why Claudio Cardinal Hummes wrote in 2007 told us that in order to obtain a new generation of holy priests, apostolic souls burning with divine fire and ready to lead the faithful onto the battlefield of the New Evangelization, we must begin perpetual Eucharistic adoration in every diocese of the world:

> Thereby—and precisely because of the place occupied and the role served by the Most Blessed Virgin in salvation history—we intend in a very particular way to entrust all Priests to Mary, the Mother of the High and Eternal Priest, bringing about in the Church a move-

ment of prayer, placing twenty-four-hour continuous Eucharistic adoration at the center, so that a prayer of adoration, thanksgiving, praise, petition, and reparation, will be raised to God, incessantly and from every corner of the earth, with the primary intention of awakening a sufficient number of holy vocations to the priestly state. . . .[8]

When Christ first gave the mission to evangelize the world to his apostles he told them "to stay in the city" until they were clothed with power from on high (Luke 24:29). The apostles understood the "city" to mean the cenacle, where Jesus had instituted the Holy Eucharist several weeks beforehand. So back they went to this place of Eucharistic grace, and united to Mary they entered into a state of constant prayer. Before long they had been filled to overflowing with all of the gifts of the Holy Spirit. So transformed were they that no power in the world could stop them from preaching. Let us also go back into the cenacle, with our rosary beads in our hands and the Bible on our laps, and we too will be clothed with power from on high to go out pierce the darkness of our world with the light of the "Eternal Gospel" of Jesus Christ (Rev 14:6).

*Rev. Sean Davidson is a member of the Missionaries of the Most Holy Eucharist, a public clerical association devoted to the spread of Eucharistic adoration in the Church.*

# Notes

**Foreword**
1. Interview, Vatican Information Service (VIS), October 16, 2012.
2. *The Catholic Church and Conversion* (San Francisco, Ignatius: 2006), 19.
3. *Apostolicam Actuositatem*, 16.
4. *Christifideles Laici*, 33.

**Chapter Two**
1. (New York, Image: 2007).

**Chapter Three**
1. Raymond Arroyo, *Mother Angelica: The Remarkable Story of a Nun, Her Nerve, and a Network of Miracles* (New York, Image Books: 2005), 14.
2. Mother M. Angelica, *Jesus My Savior*, accessed Nov 1, 2012: http://www.ewtn.com/library/mother/ma23.htm

**Chapter Ten**
1. Arthur Quiller-Couch, ed., *The Oxford Book of English Verse, 1250–1900* (Oxford: Clarendon Press, 1912), 36-37.

2. Pope Benedict XVI, Homily, Mass for the Inauguration of the Pontificate of Pope Benedict XVI (April 24, 2005), http://www.vatican.va/holy_father/benedict_xvi/homilies/documents/hf_ben-xvi_hom_20050424_inizio-pontificato_en.html. In the original Italian, Pope Benedict said that each of us is a frutto, a "fruit," of the thought of God.
3. John McHugh and Charles Callan, trans., *Catechism of the Council of Trent for Parish Priests* (Rockford, Ill.: TAN Books and Publishers, 1982), 290.
4. Decree on the Life and Ministry of Priests *Presbyterorum Ordinis* (1965), no. 13. Cf. Rev. S. M. Ferigle, "Frequent Confession," in *Homiletic & Pastoral Review* (1975).
5. David C. Leege and Thomas A. Trozzolo, "Participation in Catholic Parish Life: Religious Rites and Parish Activities in the 1980s," accessed October 13, 2012, http://icl.nd.edu/assets/39488/report3.pdf
6. Center for Applied Research in the Apostolate, "The Sacrament of Reconciliation," 57-58, accessed October 13, 2012, http://cara.georgetown.edu/CARAServices/FRStats/reconciliation.pdf
7. *Compendium* of the *Catechism of the Catholic Church* (2005), Appendix B. Cf. Canon 989 (Code of Canon Law, 1983): "After having attained the age of discretion, each of the faithful is bound by an obligation faithfully to confess serious sins at least once a year."
8. Bishop William Murphy, "Faith & New Works," *Long Island Catholic* (April 13, 2011), http://www.licatholic.org/bishops-column/faith-new-works-1

9. Archdiocese of Philadelphia, "Archdiocese of Philadelphia Launches Disciples in Mission Evangelization Program: Program Follows Highly Successful Reconciliation Weekend," accessed October 13, 2012.
10. Rev. T. Kevin Corcoran, diocesan vice chancellor, priest-secretary to Bishop Arthur J. Serratelli, and coordinator of the "Welcome to Healing" initiative, in Rich Sokerka (diocesan communications director), e-mail message to author, October 4, 2012.

**Chapter Eleven**
1. Mieczyslaw Mokrzycki, *"Le mardi était son jour préféré"* (Editions des Béatitudes, 2008), 62-68.
2. Fulton J. Sheen, *Treasure in Clay* (New York, Image Books: 1980), 196-209.
3. Pope Benedict XVI, General Audience on St Juliana of Cornillon, Nov. 17, 2010.
4. Pope John Paul II, Homily at the 45th International Eucharistic Congress in Seville, Spain, June 1993.
5. Peter-Julian Eymard, *The Real Presence* (Cleveland, Ohio: Emmanuel Publishing, 1938), 14.
6. Dina Belanger, *Autobiographie* (Quebec City, Canada: Charrier et Dugel, 1949), Vol I, 201.
7. Pope John Paul II, Letter to Mgr. Houssiau for the 750th anniversary of the Feast of Corpus Christi, June 28, 1996.
8. Claudio Cardinal Hummes, Congregation for the Clergy, "Letter for the Sanctification of Priests," Dec. 8, 2007.

# About the Author

Philip F. Lawler is founder and editor of Catholic World News (CWNews.com). He previously served as editor of *Crisis* magazine, the *Boston Pilot*, and *Catholic World Report*. Lawler is the author of six books on political and religious topics, most recently *A Call to Serve: Pope Francis and the Catholic Future* (Crossroad, 2013). His essays, book reviews, and editorial columns have appeared in over 100 newspapers around the United States and abroad.

## *You Might Also Like*

### Bernard McGinn

### The Doctors of the Church
Thirty-Three Men and Women Who Shaped Christianity

Paperback, 280 pages, 978-0-8245-2549-1

Written by one of the world's top authorities on the history of Christianity, this user-friendly resource is an introduction to thirty-three remarkable individuals who shaped our understanding of the Catholic faith.

"McGinn's portrayal of each doctor is rich, as the brief life narrative of each doctor sketches out the interplay between inspiration, institution, and context. It is the product of this interplay that becomes the means through which the doctors relate to God and their world and institutions. The information McGinn imparts about the doctors is understandably succinct yet substantive, teasing the reader to plunge more fully in the doctors' lives and thoughts. For those readers who seek brief 'pearls of wisdom,' this book delivers, liberally quoting from their writings, whether they are tomes, treatises, sermons, or letters."
—Oswald John Nira, *Spiritual Life*.

A fascinating look at the men and women who have made major contributions to Christianity, this work also tells the story of the development of Christian theology—one doctor at a time.

**The Crossroad Publishing Company**

## *You Might Also Like*

**Mitchell Kalpakgian**

**The Virtues We Need Again**
21 Life Lessons from the Great Books of the West

Paperback, 288 pages, 978-0-8245-2655-9

Books you might have sampled in school—or skipped on your college reading lists—come to life as timeless sources of wisdom about human nature, ethics, and our relationship with God. Under the expert guidance of longtime literature teacher Mitchell Kalpakgian, *The Aeneid*, the Bible, *The Divine Comedy*, *The Canterbury Tales*, the plays of Shakespeare, and works by Samuel Johnson, Nathaniel Hawthorne, the Brothers Grimm, Herman Melville, Robert Frost, and George Orwell offer readers young and old, a catalyst for personal development.

"Mitchell Kalpakgian has a unique knack for drawing out that kernel of eternal truth that gives meaning and purpose to the human experience. Take and read, and let it rekindle your wonder and joy."
—Pieter Vree, editor, *New Oxford Review*

**The Crossroad Publishing Company**

## *You Might Also Like*

**Stefan von Kempis and Philip F. Lawler**

**A Call To Serve**
Pope Francis and the Catholic Future

Paperback, 160 pages, 978-0-8245-5005-9

This thoughtful, vivid introduction to Pope Francis's life and his promising future in the Vatican details the historic events surrounding Pope Benedict XVI's resignation, the subsequent election of Pope Francis, and the particulars of the new pope's spirituality and thought. It features:

- Full color photography
- Vivid storytelling and in-depth analysis
- Insights from Pope Francis's friends, family, and even his childhood sweetheart
- Firsthand accounts of Vatican proceedings
- Reflections by Pope Francis on the heart of our faith, and his relationship with Jesus
- The daunting challenges that face the new pope

"The inside story of the recent abdication by one pope and the election of a startling new one—complete with colorful photos and analysis." —Fr. C. J. McCloskey, Church historian and Research Fellow at the Faith and Reason Institute in Washington, DC.

*Support your local bookstore or order directly
from the publisher at www.crossroadpublishing.com*

*To request a catalog or inquire about
quantity orders, please e-mail
sales@crossroadpublishing.com*

www.ingramcontent.com/pod-product-compliance
Lightning Source LLC
Chambersburg PA
CBHW011950150426
43195CB00018B/2882